Joy Jots

A special gift from

_____

_____

بسم الله الرحمن الرحيم

Joy Jots

Exercises for a Happy Heart

Tamara Gray

6/18/17

DAYBREAK PRESS

2014

Published by:
Daybreak Press
online at: daybreak.rabata.org
St. Paul, Minnesota, USA
ISBN: 978-0-9906259-1-9
Library of Congress Control Number: 2014914447

Cover design by Essma Imady
Design and typesetting by scholarlytype.com
Printed in the United States of America

Dedication

To my husband, Dr. Omar Imady

Writer, thinker, scholar, and seeker along the path. His shaikh once said about him, "If you squeeze him you will only find light."

Acknowledgements

*T*HE PROPHET ﷺ SAID, "Who does not thank people, has not thanked God." I would like to express my gratitude to Najiyah Maxfield and Anna-Maria Ramzy, who both made significant contributions to the reflection questions and projects found at the end of each essay, and Eamaan Rabbat, who assisted with research and provided the transliteration. Their creative contributions, critical questions, and detailed editing raised the book to a higher level.

Special thanks are also due to the myriads of women who read and commented on my weekly essays over the past year. Your support and enthusiasm helped bring this book to fruition.

Contents

Introduction 1

1. The Fresh Breeze of the New Year 5
2. A Friend like ʿUmar 11
3. Joy 16
4. Joy at the End 20
5. Debt to be Repaid 24
6. Give Thanks 30
7. Open Line to the Heart 35
8. Confidence 40
9. Grievances, Grudges and the
   Spiritual Standstill 44
10. Birth 49
11. The Mawlid 54
12. Ebullient Emulation 59
13. The Yearly Spreadsheet 64
14. There is Enough 71
15. Mosqued 75
16. Revert or Convert? 80
17. Love is a Verb 85
18. Who We Are and Who We Can Become:
    The Story of Banī al-Azd 90
19. Nafs Training 95
20. Fast Food or Slow-Roasted Goodness? 100
21. Fading Faith 105
22. Keeping Faith 111
23. Spring in Every Season 115
24. Soap for the Mouth .120
25. Taxes 127

26. A Simple Formula 132
27. Rajab and *Tawba* 136
28. Rajab Shopping. 142
29. Celebrate Our Many Mothers. 146
30. Messy Closets and Rajab 150
31. Bankrupt? 154
32. The Opportunity: Niṣf Shaʿbān 159
33. Our Statement of Faith 164
34. A Letter from a Friend. 169
35. A Quenching Cure. 173
36. Ramadan Rulings 179
37. Finding My Badr 184
38. The Final Paper and Exam 189
39. Colorful Celebrations 194
40. The Fasting of Shawwāl. 199
41. Avoiding the Mud 203
42. A Woman with a Voice 208
43. A Call to Speak. 212
44. Follow the Sound Waves of
    our Predecessors. 215
45. Use the Mute Button 221
46. Fight the Brain Drain. 227
47. Respect 231
48. Days of Change 236
49. The Day of ʿArafa 241
50. Eid Again! 246
51. Projections. 250
52. Feats of Felicity. 256

About the Author 261

Introduction

THE MUSLIM'S YEAR INCLUDES blessed days and times. The month of Ramadan, the days of Hajj, and the sacred months, all bring unique blessings to our lives if we take advantage of them. These seasons bring us the ability to refocus, to engage in self-reflection and to become of those who remember God at all times and places.

There are other calendar events that touch the believer's heart. The New Year makes us think about fresh starts, Thanksgiving encourages us to talk about gratefulness and Mother's Day encourages us to fulfill the Prophet's ﷺ injunction to put our mothers first.

Over the course of a year, every human being will experience great and glorious moments and downright depressing instances. Babies are born, marriages are contracted, people get sick, have accidents, and some die. In the course of one year there will be many mundane duties done and frequent errands completed. There will be days when life seems overwhelming and other days when it seems just perfect.

During all of this, we Muslims must remember one thing:

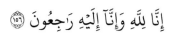

To God we belong and it is to Him that we return.
(2:156)

Remembering this great and lofty principle is easier said than done. When you are knee deep in laundry, the baby is crying, the toddler is in the cupboard, you are not dressed and it is 4:00 pm, it is hard to think elevated thoughts.

When your sister is getting a divorce, you have the flu and your computer is on the blink, it is a challenge to stay focused.

When your ten-year-old refuses to make *wuḍū᾿*, your teenager has a secret twitter account and your husband is rarely home, it is easy to panic.

When you are buying a house, considering a new job and reveling in a clean bill of health, it can be easy to choose a chocolate cake for celebration and neglect charity and prayer.

There is great danger in living a life of heedlessness that is lacking in self-reflection. Allah ﷻ tells us of the words that will be spoken by one who did not pay attention to his life:

$$ يَقُولُ يَٰلَيْتَنِى قَدَّمْتُ لِحَيَاتِى ﴿٢٤﴾ $$

He will say, "O! I wish I sent ahead [some good] for my life." (89:24)

We do not want to be of those who stagnate and suffer in this life and the next. We want to be people of joy. Allah ﷻ tells us that the people of happiness and success are those who have *taqwā* and

$$ ٱلَّذِينَ يُؤْمِنُونَ بِٱلْغَيْبِ وَيُقِيمُونَ ٱلصَّلَوٰةَ وَمِمَّا رَزَقْنَٰهُمْ يُنفِقُونَ ﴿٣﴾ وَٱلَّذِينَ يُؤْمِنُونَ بِمَآ أُنزِلَ إِلَيْكَ وَمَآ أُنزِلَ مِن $$

قَبْلِكَ وَبِٱلْأَخِرَةِ هُمْ يُوقِنُونَ ۝ أُوْلَٰٓئِكَ عَلَىٰ هُدًى مِّن رَّبِّهِمْ وَأُوْلَٰٓئِكَ هُمُ ٱلْمُفْلِحُونَ ۝

Who believe in the unseen, establish prayer, and spend out of what We have provided for them, and who believe in what has been revealed to you, and what was revealed before you, and of the Hereafter, they are certain. Those are upon [right] guidance from their Lord, and it is those who are the successful (al-mufliḥūn). (2:3-5)

Reading one essay a week, pondering on the reflection and engaging in the project will walk you through a variety of spiritual conundrums and personal challenges and guide you toward a spiritual joy that abides regardless of your external circumstances. Just as the Prophet ﷺ assigned the Muhājirīn and the Anṣār as helpers one to another, I hope to reach from the pages of this book and take your hand. Hand in hand, all of us together will move through the year, meeting our challenges and celebrating our accomplishments and praising Allah all the while. May Allah ﷻ grant us *tawfīq* (serendipitous fortune), deep faith and a bond that holds us up and gives us focus and energy. *Āmīn.*

Joy Jots

Exercises for a Happy Heart

Week 1

The Fresh Breeze of
the New Year

HE FIRST LEAF THAT turns bright purple, the first snowflake that falls, and the first bright yellow daffodil that peeks its way out of crystal white snow – their newness takes the breath away.

The new Islamic year comes to us unblemished by sin, unmarked by tragedy and unspoiled in its possibilities. It is a fresh breeze that comes to blow away despair and frustration. It is a new chapter. It is a new chance.

In January, people will make resolutions, join gyms, buy books, and cut up their credit cards. The concept of a resolution is also relevant to the month of Muḥarram, as it is a month of *tawba* (repentance) and forgiveness.

The month of Muḥarram is the month in which the *hijra* began. In the dead of night, the Muslims snuck quietly out of Mecca, leaving behind their homes, property, and family members. They risked their health to obey the Prophet ﷺ. They left behind their houses because a new home for the fledgling community was to be raised in Yathrib – City of the Prophet ﷺ. They went on *hijra* to join with the waiting Anṣār and build a new *umma*. They went forth in commitment to a belief in One God and His prophet. They went forth in absolute *tawakkul* (trust)

– the *tawakkul* that includes full effort and complete conviction in the Grace of God. They went forth bringing their whole selves and their whole lives to Allah ﷻ.

In the month of Muḥarram, centuries before, Moses was granted victory over Pharaoh; belief in One God triumphed over idolatry and human arrogance. Fasting on this day, which is called the day of ʿĀshūrāʾ, is a confirmed *sunna*, and the beloved companion ʿAmr b. al ʿĀs ؓ would say, "Who fasts the day of ʿĀshūrāʾ, it is as though he fasted an entire year, and who gives charity on the day of ʿĀshūrāʾ, it is as though he gave charity for an entire year." Thus, Muslims celebrate the day of ʿĀshūrāʾ in fasting and good works.

In this year, let us hold in our mind's eye the *hijra* and ʿĀshūrāʾ. Let us begin the year clinging to belief, soaked in *tawakkul*, and in victory over our sin and spiritual deficiencies. Let us begin our resolutions now, and not wait for January. Let us make our own spiritual *hijra*.

The *hijra* of Prophet Muhammad ﷺ had three components:

1. A goal: get the Muslim community safely to Medina.

2. A plan: the Prophet ﷺ laid an elaborate plan that included stealth, strategy, and the blessing of God.

3. A companion: Abū Bakr ؓ was chosen as the Prophet's companion on his ﷺ *hijra*, and he fulfilled his role with vigilance and joy. Indeed, it is said that Abū Bakr ؓ first felt what was meant by 'tears of joy' when the Prophet ﷺ told him he would be his companion on the road.

Our spiritual *hijra* also must have a goal, a plan, and at least one companion.

Goals

1. *Farḍ* prayers: From day one to the end of the year, let us commit to not missing a single *farḍ* prayer. Let us make *hijra* from the comfort of our beds and self-consciousness at work and school to the joy and confidence of prayer.

2. *Tahajjud*: the *tahajjud* revolution is in full swing with more and more women waking up for *tahajjud* across the world. Prayer at night is an essential part of the worship life of the believer. Allah ﷻ speaks to us in *Sūrat al-Insān*, where we are told to spend the night in prostration and glorifying Him:

$$ وَمِنَ ٱلَّيْلِ فَٱسْجُدْ لَهُۥ وَسَبِّحْهُ لَيْلًا طَوِيلًا ﴿٢٦﴾ $$

And of the night, prostrate yourself to Him, and glorify Him during the long night. (76:26)

In *Sūrat al-Isrāʾ*, Allah ﷻ is very specific about the necessity of this *sunna* prayer:

$$ وَمِنَ ٱلَّيْلِ فَتَهَجَّدْ بِهِۦ نَافِلَةً لَّكَ عَسَىٰٓ أَن يَبْعَثَكَ رَبُّكَ مَقَامًا مَّحْمُودًا ﴿٧٩﴾ $$

And rise from sleep during the night – it is an additional prayer for you. Perhaps your Lord will raise you to an honored position. (17:79)

Raise us to an honored position... indeed the Muslim *umma* is in dire need of this. Let this year be the year where Muslims are raised to an honored position through our *tahajjud*.

3. Behavior: Muʿādh b. Jabal ؓ said, "The last instruction I received from the Prophet ﷺ when I put

7

my foot in the stirrup was, "Beautify your manners for the people, O Mu'ādh b. Jabal!'" (*Muwaṭṭa' al-Imām Mālik*)

»أحسِن خلقك للناس يا معاذ بن جبل«.

Let this be a year without slamming doors and screaming voices. Let us learn to 'be the change we want to see in the world.' In our homes, let us be the instigators of joy and happiness. In our communities, let us think of creative ways to coax Muslims back into the mosque (perhaps we first need to find out where it is!). In the wider community, let us be of those whose very presence reminds others of God and His prophets.

In every season of this year, let us embrace beauty. When the first snowflake falls, let it find us out from under thick comforters and standing in prayer at night. When spring flowers dance in the breeze, let our voices be reciting Quran. When the summer sun warms our backs, let us be warming the hearts of others. And when fall comes again, and the leaves change to purple, gold, and bright-flaming red, let us be of those whose prayers remain green and strong – let it be that not a single obligatory prayer has been missed. Then when next year shows its innocent face, let us put this year in our book of deeds without regret, but with hope. Hope for our *umma*, hope for our families, and hope for our very selves.

Happy New Year, everyone. May it be truly joyful.

Reflection

Did I miss any *farḍ* prayers last year? How many? What can I do to make sure it does not happen this year?

Project

During the course of your year with this journal, you will be embarking on a journey of spiritual growth.

Everyone meets different obstacles on their journey; some of it will come blessedly easy for you, like coasting on a downhill slope, and other parts will prove more difficult, like trudging up a craggy mountain. But there is one thing that will help you keep going and growing: fuel. The fuel that will give you the ability to meet each obstacle, overcome each slump and achieve real progress is *tahajjud*. *Tahajjud* opens internal doors, provides unique insights, and waters the tender shoots of our awakening souls. It is the keystone habit of the seeker. If you have not joined the *tahajjud* revolution already, make this the week you begin! And welcome to the sisterhood of women all over the world who are being invited by Allah to this beautiful practice of the *ṣaḥāba* (companions of the Prophet).

Tips

1. Set a goal of rising fifteen minutes before Fajr, making *wuḍūʾ*, and praying two *rakʿas* before the *adhān*.
2. Success doesn't just happen! Make it as easy as possible to succeed by planning ahead. Here are some tips to help you out:
   a) Read about the importance of *tahajjud*.
   b) Find a *tahajjud* buddy.
   c) Go to bed early.
   d) Get a special wake-up alarm. There are *tahajjud* alarm apps for both Android and iPhone.
   e) Remember that while it might be difficult at first, soon you will come to value it as your special, quiet prayer and rejuvenating time.

Reflection / Project

Week 2

A Friend like ʿUmar

THE ROAD FROM MECCA to Medina was fraught with hardship. It was a desert path, with little in the way of safety or comfort. During the *hijra* from Mecca to Medina, it was a dangerous road where enemies could be lying in wait or following in the *muhājir's* tracks.

It is narrated in *Sīrat Ibn Hishām* that ʿĀyyāsh b. Abī Rabīʿa and ʿUmar b. al-Khaṭṭāb ﷺ met outside of Mecca and traveled together the long road from Mecca to Medina. One wonders what they spoke of, if they were afraid, if they knew who was tracking them and quickly catching up to them.

At the outskirts of Medina, having reached their destination to relative safety, Abū Jahl b. Hishām and his brother, al-Ḥārith b. Hishām, caught up with them. "ʿAyyāsh! Indeed your mother has vowed that a comb will not touch her head until she sees you, and she will not shade herself from the sun until she sees you."

ʿAyyāsh pitied his mother, and began to consider returning. ʿUmar ﷺ saw through the ruse and said to him, "O ʿAyyāsh, indeed by God, your people want not but to tempt you away from your religion – so be forewarned. For, by God, if your mother were to be afflicted with lice, she would comb her hair, and if the heat of Mecca intensifies upon her, she will seek shade."

11

ʿAyyāsh began to see other benefits in returning to Mecca. He said, "I shall release her of her vow, and I have some money there which I will lay hold of."

ʿUmar, in an impressive act of brotherhood, said, "By God, you know that I am of the richest of Quraish, and I will give you half of my money if you do not go with them!"

ʿAyyāsh still insisted on going.

ʿUmar, in a last-ditch attempt to save him from capture, said, "If you insist, then take my camel. It is well bred and docile; do not dismount it. If you suspect your people of trickery, escape upon it."

ʿUmar ﷺ offered ʿAyyāsh his friendship, financial support, and a means of escape.

ʿAyyāsh took his camel, but after they had gone for a while along the road, Abū Jahl said to him, "By God, my brother (they were half-brothers), riding upon my camel has become harsh. Will you not let me ride your camel?"

ʿAyyāsh made his camel kneel, and he was attacked, shackled, and bound. In Mecca they tormented him until he succumbed, as Hishām b. al-ʿĀṣ had done before him.

Later, when the verses of acceptance and forgiveness regarding those who had been imprisoned and had succumbed were revealed, ʿUmar wrote them down with his own hand and sent them to his companion.

The danger of the *hijra* was real and serious. ʿUmar ﷺ set an example of the type of companion we need to help us through. Even when ʿAyyāsh made all the wrong decisions, ʿUmar remained his friend and caring companion, hoping for his release and success.

Our *hijra* is not the *hijra* of geography, but rather an internal *hijra*. It, too, is fraught with dangers and enemies. As we embark upon our *hijra* from

❀ ignorance to knowledge

❀ heedlessness (*ghafla*) to remembrance (*dhikr*)

- distance from Allah ﷻ to closeness to Him and His pleasure
- distance from the beloved Prophet ﷺ to closeness to him ﷺ and love for him ﷺ
- toxic people to nourishing people
- stinginess (material and emotional) to generosity
- shallowness to depth
- wasted time to full days and nights
- laziness to energy
- aimlessness to focus
- despair to hope

'Umar ﷺ was supportive, respectful, and thoughtful. He offered money and property. He never gave up on his friend, even in his darkest hour.

If we are to succeed in our spiritual *hijra*, we need friends like 'Umar ﷺ. And if our communities are to succeed, we need to be a friend like 'Umar.

Whatever the spiritual journey, let this be the year of success. Let this be the year we emigrate together from whatever dark place we find ourselves in, to a place of light.

Reflection

Read the project first this week.

Write about the spiritual goals you are asking Allah to help you with this year. What charity did you perform in the name of those goals, and what happened when you did?

Project

With this journal, you are embarking on a *hijra* from whatever spiritual state you are in now to a "new and improved" one. You will see trials, face obstacles, marvel over miracles, and feel your "*ʿibāda* (worship) muscles" strengthen and tone. You will learn new things, feel new feelings, and reach new heights.

When we are traveling the spiritual road, charity is key. Choose one act of charity to perform this week. It could be, for example, donating money, babysitting your neighbor's children, or volunteering at a nursing home. Whatever you choose, do it with the intention of pleasing Allah and beginning your spiritual *hijra*.

Reflection / Project

_____

_____

_____

_____

_____

_____

_____

_____

_____

_____

_____

_____

_____

_____

_____

_____

_____

_____

_____

_____

_____

_____

_____

Week 3

Joy

THE WORD JOY IS one of my favorite words. We can use it to say things like, "She cried tears of joy!" or, "At that moment, she was soaking in the joy of being alive." In its verb form we say, "Rejoice!" as an adjective, "She uttered a joyful noise!" and as an adverb, "The children giggled joyously."

Sometimes I think we come to Islam thinking it is better to be miserable. We carry around a 'martyr's attitude.' This is not the martyr who struggles and fights and dies in the way of God. No. This is the whining and complaining 'poor-me' martyr.

Poor me! I have to live in a small apartment; poor me, I have to clean a big house; poor me, I'm not married; poor me, I'm married; poor me, I have only one child; poor me, I don't have any children; poor me, I have so many children; poor me, I have to do the dishes every day; poor me, I have to go to work; poor me, I can't work… and it goes on and on and on.

Every life, in essence, is the same. All have great and wonderful moments and all have trials. The only difference is in our *riḍā* (contentment) of this life, this stage of life, this moment.

Ibn al-Qayyim tells us of two ways that *ḥuzn* (grief/sadness/sorrow) is mentioned in the Quran. It is forbidden in the verse:

$$\text{وَلَا تَهِنُوا۟ وَلَا تَحْزَنُوا۟}$$

Do not weaken and do not grieve, (3:139)

and it is rejected in the verse:

$$\text{وَلَا خَوْفٌ عَلَيْهِمْ وَلَا هُمْ يَحْزَنُونَ ۝}$$

No fear shall afflict them, nor shall they grieve. (2:274)

This is not the natural grief of loss, but a grief that overcomes the spirit. It is most beloved to Shaiṭān that the believer suffers in grief and depression so that it throws him off course and stops him in his tracks.

Indeed, the Prophet ﷺ sought refuge from grief, saying, *"O Allah, I seek refuge in you from worry and grief."* (Saḥīḥ al-Bukhārī)

$$\text{«اللّهمَّ إنِّي أعوذُ بِكَ مِنَ الهَمِّ والحزَنِ.»}$$

It is thus that Ibn al-Qayyim says, "Depression/grief weakens the heart, dampens one's resolve and erodes one's will, and there is nothing more pleasing to Shaiṭān than the sorrow of a believer. So rejoice! Spread cheer! Be positive and think good of Allah ﷻ. Trust in Him and rely on Him. Indeed, you will find happiness and deep contentment in all circumstances."

This is an awesome, joyful faith. Every day should have a joy jot – or something that brings you enough joy that it needs to be written down. Bring joy to others, rejoice, spread joy. You are a Muslim. That is a joyful word in and of itself. Let it be your first joy jot. "I am a Muslim... *Al-ḥamdu l-i-Llāh!*"

Reflection

What brings me joy? How can I go about extending that joy to others?

Project

Joy Jots. Jot down one thing that gives you joy in each of the coming days this week.

Reflection / Project

_____

_____

_____

_____

_____

_____

_____

_____

_____

_____

_____

_____

_____

_____

_____

_____

_____

_____

_____

_____

_____

_____

Week 4

Joy at the End

THE CHEROKEE SAY,
"When you were born,
you cried and the world rejoiced.
Live your life so that when you die,
the world cries and you rejoice."

Riding down an elevator, I was in a hurry. Hurry up! Lots of things to do! So much to get done before I travel! I was leaving my second appointment (after having taught school all day!) and already thinking about what was next on the agenda. My friend handed me her iPhone, "Have you seen this?" she asked me.

I held in my hand a picture of one of the most beautiful, joyful expressions I have ever seen in my life. With eyes squinted in welcome, lips pursed in a smile of joy, and cheeks crinkled with happy lines of a lifetime – the face said, "Finally!" It said, "I've missed you." It said, "Oh! How I've longed to see you – and look! You are right here!" I could hear the joy in the voice that was to come from that expression. Little gurgles of bubbling jubilation and murmurs of content bounced off the picture and into my consciousness. I smelled flowers. Not roses – no, not the scent of heavy perfume – jasmine and honeysuckle surrounded me as I imagined they surrounded him.

The picture jolted me out of my reverie of 'busy' and brought me into the present. "How beautiful!" I said.

"Yes," my friend replied. "That is Shaikh al-Kurdī (the shaikh of Quran who has granted thousands of *ijāzas* over the past twenty years). The picture was taken right after his death."

Right after his death? I looked again. This was indeed extraordinary. I have heard tell of smiles on the faces of the dead, pleasant looks, fingers that stood up in attestation to the oneness of God... but this was something else. His face shone. His face radiated light and gladness. *Mā shāʾ Allah.*

Our Prophet ﷺ says, "...When a believer nears death, an angel comes to him from Allah ﷻ bearing glad tidings of what awaits him – and there is nothing more beloved to him than that he will meet his Lord – and Allah loves to meet him..." (*Majmaʿ al-Zawāʾid*)

»المؤمن إذا حضر جاءه البشير من الله فليس شيء أحب من أن يكون قد لقي الله فأحب الله لقاءه.«

Ḥusn al-Khitām – an ending that is good. This is the goal of all Muslims. We all want to meet Allah ﷻ with our prayers prayed, our fasts fasted, and our deeds good and plentiful. God forbid that we die on a day of a missed prayer, on a day of telling a lie, on a day of sin. We want to die with our mothers, fathers, spouses and teachers pleased with us. When we die, we do not want anyone's heart to be heavy toward us. We want to end this ultimate test with an excellent grade – we want to go to God pleased and having pleased.

I have a theory. As I look at how many 'endings' we have in life – end of the school year, end of a season, end of an era, end of a project, end of a book, end of a meal, end of Ramadan, end of Hajj, end of... I begin to see them all as practice and pattern building. In one way or another, life is a series of projects. We must continuously and intentionally complete each project at the top of our game.

If we wish to have *ḥusn al-khitām*, we need to perfect our daily, weekly, yearly and seasonal endings. We must strive to complete projects; when changing jobs, we must complete the first one as though we were staying forever. We must avoid 'petering out', stay away from despair, and never allow pessimism to make final decisions for us.

My theory is that if we work hard to create *ḥusn al-khitām* in our daily lives, Allah ﷻ will bless us with it at the end of our lives.

May we be of those whose faces glow with joy and peace when we find ourselves at the end of a long and beautiful life. May we be of those who lived our lives, every little beginning and every little ending, for the sake of Allah ﷻ and in service to His religion, His prophet and all of His beloved creation.

Reflection

What are some projects that you would like to have completed by the end of your life? Are there any steps you can take to begin working toward them now?

Project

Find three shorter term projects that need completion now and set a goal of getting them finished (or at least making good progress on them!) within the next month. Quantify your goals and make the steps reasonable, so you can track your progress and feel a sense of achievement.

Reflection / Project

Week 5

Debt to be Repaid

WHEN I WAS A young girl, the day before a road trip was always 'library day'. It was the day we gathered all the library books in the house and returned them to the library. As an adult, and as a Muslim, every trip I take (and there have been many over the past 30 years) includes a day or two of 'returns'. Pyrex dishes returned to owners, books and movies returned to owners, and all bills paid. I do this because taking any trip makes me think of endings. I do not want to die away from home, but if I do, at least I do not want to die in debt.

Our debt to Allah ﷻ is defined by missing obligations. Some people owe zakat that they have not paid, others owe fasting days that have not been made up, and still others owe a hajj, but the primary debt carried by Muslims is the debt of missed prayers.

It is the glory of the Muslims that we pray five times a day. We stand, we recite, we glorify, we praise, we plead, we bow, we prostrate... It is a beautiful prayer.

It is a prayer that we *must* offer. If missed, it is not 'no big deal', but rather a debt that must be repaid.

If we hope to die in peace and joy, we must pay back our debt to Allah ﷻ. We must do it meticulously. Just like a bank record of deposits, each prayer should be recorded until the goal is reached.

There are three ways that a person might miss prayers:

1. A convert who did not pray for all of the years before she came to Islam: These missed prayers do not count against her and are not a debt weighing her down. They do not have to be made up (happy dance, all converts!).

2. A born Muslim who spent a period of time away from obedience to God and thus was not praying: These are considered prayers missed without excuse. They are a heavy burden and an oppressive debt. Ibn Taimiyya's view is that the sin is so great that the prayer cannot be made up. Imām al-Shāfi'ī holds that one should preoccupy herself with nothing else but that which keeps her alive of eating, sleeping and working, during the making-up time. Other scholars allow for a slightly more lenient approach. Indeed, for one to work for *ḥusn al-khitām*, she should set her sights on making her prayers up as quickly as possible. I know one woman who made up thirty years of prayers in the last seven years of her life. When she died, she did so with a smile on her face.

3. If you are a practicing Muslim, you might miss a prayer out of forgetfulness or sleep. The sin of this is less than the one who deliberately does not pray, but one must realize that the missing of this prayer is an indication that something is wrong in her life. There is always a reason for a missed prayer – one must seek the true and deeper reason in order to avoid more missed prayers and – God forbid – a life that ends with a prayer or more that have not been prayed. The scholars agree in this case that the prayer must be made up immediately. For one who has missed one prayer, it is necessary to pray it straightaway. So if you wake up and find that the sun has risen and you have not woken up for the

Fajr prayer, you must jump out of bed – straight to *wuḍū* and straight to the prayer carpet. Do not stop to make coffee. Do not stop to have a bite to eat. And definitely do NOT go to work or school first, thinking, "I'll do it when I get home."

The missing of a single prayer, or a series of prayers, is a serious occurrence in one's life. It must cause us to pause, to reflect, to make *tawba* for that which has stopped us from the prayer. We have all heard stories of the one who 'prayed Fajr then died' or 'prayed ʿAṣr, then died' or 'died in his prayer'… What we do not hear are the many stories of those who died having missed a prayer, or having delayed a prayer. We do not speak of these events because it is not appropriate to speak ill of the dead. If we strive toward *ḥusn al-khitām*, however, it means we must be ever aware and striving to pray our prayers at the beginning of the time – and when circumstances prevent that, we must at least intend to pray the next prayer as soon as the time comes in. So if the *adhān* for Ẓuhr is called, make the intention of prayer immediately, then pray as soon as you can. If the Angel of Death arrives before you get a chance to pray, you will have at least intended to.

Indeed, if you are close to menstruating, you will want to make an extra effort to pray on time. For if the time of Ẓuhr arrives and you can still pray, but you delay the prayer till later, and by that time you are menstruating and can no longer pray, that prayer is still *farḍ* upon you, yet you have to wait seven to ten days to pray it. God forbid that the Angel of Death visits you during that time, while you wait to pray the prayer that waits for you.

If the Angel of Death arrives before you get a chance to pray, you will at least have made the intention. *Ḥusn al-Khitām*: may it be the kind of end we are all blessed with, *Āmīn*.

Reflection

Think of the last prayer you missed. What was the immediate cause (meaning what did you prioritize over the prayer)?

What do you think might be the deeper reason? Is there something you need to make *tawba* from? Revisit this reflection if you ever miss a prayer in the upcoming year.

Project

Calculate how many prayers you have to make up and start doing so today! Choose a time each day when you will pray your *qaḍā* (make up) prayers and write it here; maybe one after each current prayer, a day's worth at *tahajjud* time each morning, or a couple between Maghrib and ʿIshā. Use the Qaḍā Prayers Chart on the next page to keep track of the prayers you have made up. If you have more than one year to make up, you can photocopy this chart, or make your own. A little at a time will get the job done.

Qaḍā' Prayers Chart (1 Year)

Week	Fajr	Ẓuhr	ʿAṣr	Maghrib	ʿIshā'
1					
2					
3					
4					
5					
6					
7					
8					
9					
10					
11					
12					
13					
14					
15					
16					
17					
18					
19					
20					
21					
22					
23					
24					
25					
26					
27					
28					
29					
30					
31					
32					
33					
34					
35					
36					
37					
38					
39					
40					
41					
42					
43					
44					
45					
46					
47					
48					
49					
50					
51					
52					

Reflection / Project

Week 6

Give Thanks

T IS THANKSGIVING WEEK in the USA and we are all thinking about what it means to be thankful. As families prepare feasts to share, and stores and malls prepare sales to lure in mobs of people who will come storming in on Friday, I observe and think. What does it really mean to be a thankful person?

Shukr (thankfulness) is a spiritual state to be sought. Allah ﷻ says:

$$فَٱتَّقُوا۟ ٱللَّهَ لَعَلَّكُمْ تَشْكُرُونَ ۝$$

Have taqwā *of God that you may be grateful.* (3:123)

The experience and clarity of that deep thankfulness is not achieved without a measure of God-consciousness. He ﷻ says:

$$وَإِذْ تَأَذَّنَ رَبُّكُمْ لَئِن شَكَرْتُمْ لَأَزِيدَنَّكُمْ ۖ وَلَئِن كَفَرْتُمْ إِنَّ عَذَابِى لَشَدِيدٌ ۝$$

And [remember] when your Lord proclaimed, "If you are grateful, I will surely increase you [in favor]; but if you deny, indeed, My punishment is severe." (14:7)

We as human beings have a tendency to forget our blessings, and we have a tendency to focus on what we do not have. We recognize it when it is missing, and quickly take it for granted again when it reappears. So our health is sorely missed in the middle of the flu, but easily forgotten in the middle of a lonely day when all we can think about is how people are not treating us right.

A great percentage of our problems could be eradicated if we learned to focus on what we have instead of what we do not have. If we were people of *shukr*, we would be people of fewer problems.

Shukr is a state to be striven toward, and it includes three pillars: knowledge, state of being, and hard work.

Knowledge is the recognition of our blessings. We live most of our life oblivious to the blessings we live with. Some even begin to believe that their blessings are their 'rights'. We must remember that all of our blessings are privileges and gifts. The refrigerator with a carton of milk that we can replenish whenever it empties, the computer, the car, the shoes, the spoons, the cereal, the sheets, the pillows, the books, the toothpaste... on and on and on – all privileges and not rights. Yet we become crabby and sullen if we do not get our daily dose of these blessings. The beginning of thankfulness is seeing each and every one of these things as a great blessing from God and appreciating every one. Can you go to the bathroom without a catheter? Can you see the phone in your hand? Can you raise your arms above your head? Can you leave your house without fear of being shot? Can you turn off the lights, close your eyes, and listen to quiet (as opposed to a buzzing or ringing in your ears)? Then you are living with – drowning in – great and powerful blessings. Take nothing for granted.

A *shukr* state of being is the feeling in the heart that is a result of knowing one's blessings. We must work on developing this state of thankfulness. Fight off bitterness and turn away from self-pity. We must be thankful to the One who blessed us before being thankful for the blessing itself. Joy in Him is before joy in anything else.

Hard work is the using of every limb in the obedience of Allah ﷻ. Because whoever thanks Allah with her tongue should not be using that same tongue for *ghība (gossip)*, *namīma (defamation)* or to hurt any part of creation.

Thankfulness of the tongue is using it for praise and remembrance and calling to Allah. Thankfulness of the eyes is to avoid looking at *ḥaram* things or the imperfections of others, and to use them instead for that which pleases Allah – like reading Qur'an, opening them at night in worship, etc. Each limb has deeds to do so that it might join the chorus of thankfulness.

On Thursday there will be many, many people in the USA thanking God for food and family. I will be one of them, as I eat and pray thankful prayers with my family. Together we will join the chorus of thankfulness, and I will observe and watch and contemplate what it means to be a thankful person.

On Thanksgiving, when people across the USA settle into a thankful state of mind, let us contemplate our blessings. Let us really and truly see them. Let us play a 'thank you' game and attempt to list the myriads of things we are thankful for. Then let us focus on the source of these blessings. Thank you, God. *Al-ḥamdu l-i-Llāh!* All praise and thanks are to You! Let us bow down in a collective *sujūd al-shukr* (prostration of thankfulness) as we let our bitterness dissipate and open our hearts to joy. Finally, let us examine our limbs and our senses, release them from the shackles of 'too busy to help and volunteer' and give them the gift of grateful service in God's cause. With knowledge, the correct state of mind, and hard work we will truly become of those who are thankful. Yā

Shakūr. We thank You.

Reflection

What are fifteen things I am thankful for? What are some blessings I take for granted? How can I move those in the latter list to the former?

Project

Thankful Hands
Allah tells us in Sūrat Yā Sīn:

$$ٱلْيَوْمَ نَخْتِمُ عَلَىٰٓ أَفْوَٰهِهِمْ وَتُكَلِّمُنَآ أَيْدِيهِمْ وَتَشْهَدُ
أَرْجُلُهُم بِمَا كَانُوا۟ يَكْسِبُونَ ۝$$

That Day, We will seal over their mouths, and their hands will speak to Us, and their feet will testify about what they used to earn. (36:65)

This week, express your thankfulness to the Sustainer and strengthen the joy in the testimony of your hands and feet by choosing one deed to perform out of sheer thankfulness. Visit someone who is ill, volunteer at a hospital or a school, offer to drive an elderly neighbor somewhere. It does not have to be a huge deed – in fact, it is better if it is small enough for you to continue it, as the Prophet ﷺ says, "The most beloved of deeds to Allah ﷻ are those that are done consistently, even if they are small." (*Ṣaḥīḥ Muslim*)

$$«أحبّ الأعمال إلى الله تعالى أدومها وإن قلّ.»$$

33

Reflection / Project

_____

_____

_____

_____

_____

_____

_____

_____

_____

_____

_____

_____

_____

_____

_____

_____

_____

_____

_____

_____

_____

_____

_____

_____

_____

Week 7

Open Line to the Heart

N EAR OF CORN holds so many kernels that each bite pops several of the sweet pouches into your mouth.

A frozen river reflects the scenery around it in waves of color and tufts of snow that crinkle the smile lines of your eyes.

Expensive perfume tip-toes around you for hours after you have left it on the shelf.

A mother's voice changes your mood and calms your nerves.

And the smooth, cool feel of the black stone changes your heart at the moment of contact.

فَبِأَيِّ ءَالَآءِ رَبِّكُمَا تُكَذِّبَانِ ﴿١٣﴾

Which of the blessings of your Lord do you deny? (55:13)

Our senses are blessings that give us the ability to experience other blessings. Day after day we see, hear, smell, taste and touch things that bring us joy, sustenance and love.

Our heart is attached to each of these senses.

When our eyes gaze upon beauty, our heart is lifted. Beauty in a rolling mountain, a tree with its branches iced and sparkling, or a single snowflake magnified thousands of times gives us hope, releases constriction, and offers the calming reminder of the Hand of God. Gazing upon people of God brings us to a state of *dhikr* (remembrance of God), and we are calmed in their presence and our minds gain clarity.

But when we allow our eyes to look at that which is *ḥarām*, whether on television, an Internet game or an inappropriate website, our heart suffers the damage.

The same senses that can take us closer to Allah ﷻ can prevent us from ever reaching Him.

The Prophet ﷺ himself turned the face of al-Faḍl b. al-ʿAbbās so that he would not gaze at a woman who came to ask the Prophet ﷺ for a ruling.

Abdullah b. al-ʿAbbās ﵎ narrates: "Al-Faḍl b. al-ʿAbbās rode behind Allah's Messenger ﷺ as his companion rider on the back portion of his she-camel on the day of Naḥr (slaughtering of sacrifice, 10th of Dhū al-Ḥijja) and al-Faḍl was a handsome man. The Prophet ﷺ stopped to give the people verdicts [regarding their matters].

A beautiful woman from the tribe of Khaitham came, asking the verdict of Allah's Messenger. Al-Faḍl started looking at her, as her beauty attracted him. The Prophet ﷺ looked behind while al-Faḍl was looking at her, so the Prophet ﷺ held out his hand backwards and caught the chin of al-Faḍl and turned his face in order that he should not gaze at her..." (*Saḥīḥ al-Bukhārī*)

The Prophet ﷺ was teaching al-Faḍl how to behave – not to stare in lust at a woman. In today's sexually charged society, images appear in front of us every day. They appear in front of our family members, too. It is up to us to set the environment at home as an environment of purity. Help yourself and your family members protect their eyes.

Your senses are in your care. Let your eyes gaze at beauty, and protect them from that which brings ugliness to your heart. Let your ears listen to Quran and beautiful words, and protect them from the cacophony of sin and disbelief. Let your nose breathe deeply of clean, fresh smells, and train your spirit to smell of good deeds and not of sin. Let your hands hold the hands of your family, neighbors and friends, such that they do not fall into mistakes in idleness. And let your tongue taste the sweetness of faith, and not relegate your heart and soul to hellfire with hearsay and gossip.

Senses are blessings to help us experience our blessings, and they are a direct line to our hearts. Protect your sense of sight, hearing, smell, touch and taste with obedience and good works.

May Allah protect us from that which we cannot avoid.

Reflection

Which senses do you have the most trouble protecting?

Project

People often believe that, though they watch or listen to *harām* things, they are not affected. They watch unmarried couples kissing or people drinking alcohol on TV and think that they are immune to the ill effects of those images, that that value system does not damage their spirit. People listen to music that features *harām* subject matter and assume that their hearts are somehow protected. Those same people would never eat a salad with bacon bits on it, thinking, "It's just a *little* pork. It won't hurt me." Yet seeing or hearing *harām* things is just as dangerous as eating pork. This week, try to protect every avenue by which *harām* could enter your body.

Tips

a. Eyes: "Watch" what you see on TV. Don't indulge in things that feature nudity or alcohol, for example.

b. Ears: Avoid cursing, whether it be in music or from friends who may think that sort of thing to be "no big deal."

c. Nose: Practice being humble and not turning your nose up at others.

d. Hands: Make sure yours are not being tight-fisted or holding others back.

e. Tongue: Steer it clear of backbiting, cursing or harsh words.

Reflection / Project

Week 8

Confidence

THERE ARE OVER SEVEN billion people in the world, and at any given time someone is happy and joyful while another is suffering and in pain.

Allah ﷻ created us and created this *dunyā*. He placed within it His laws. Part and parcel of His laws is that Janna is a place of reward and perfection, but this *dunyā* is not. Here on earth we find sickness, cruelty, cold, hunger, oppression, pain, natural disasters and unnatural accidents. Someone, somewhere, is crying right now. Someone else is hurting. Someone else is silently suffering in pain.

Allah knows exactly who is crying. He knows who is hurting. He knows who is lonely and afraid.

When Allah (may He be glorified) created us, the angels said to Him:

أَتَجْعَلُ فِيهَا مَن يُفْسِدُ فِيهَا وَيَسْفِكُ ٱلدِّمَآءَ وَنَحْنُ نُسَبِّحُ بِحَمْدِكَ وَنُقَدِّسُ لَكَ

Will You place upon it one who causes corruption therein and sheds blood, while we declare Your praise and sanctify You? (2:30)

Angels do not go against Allah's will, yet they wondered at this strange new creation, a creation that would choose. Allah ﷻ responded:

$$\text{قَالَ إِنِّي أَعْلَمُ مَا لَا تَعْلَمُونَ ۞}$$

Indeed, I know that which you do not know. (2:30)

Then He proceeded to teach Adam the names of all things.

When we were created and given knowledge and sent to live upon this earth, it was in love. We are the representatives (*khalīfa*) of Allah ﷻ, and in our ability to choose lies the other side of this *dunyā*.

Abdullah b. al-Mubārak relates, "Once, while I was in Mecca, we were struck with a severe drought. It had not rained for weeks and all the people gathered at the *masjid* to pray for rain. I was also amongst them, sitting next to the gate of Banū Sā'iba. An Abyssinian slave wearing tattered garments came and sat in front of me. I could hear him praying, 'O Allah, bad deeds and sinning have frayed the faces and You have stopped showering us with Your Mercy to teach humanity a lesson. I ask you *Yā Ḥalīm, Yā Raḥīm, Yā* the One whose people know nothing from except good, send rain unto us this moment.' He prayed until the clouds appeared and it rained." The story goes on to tell how Abdullah b. al-Mubārak ran after him to learn more about him and finally purchased him in order to free him and serve him. The slave died before that could happen, and of his last words were, "Life was good when the secret was between my Lord and me. Now you know, and then someone else will come to know. Now I am no longer in need of this life."

Here on earth we find those who choose to reach out to the ill and make them comfortable; we find kind people who soothe broken hearts; we find people who feed the hungry – those hungry of body and those hungry of soul. We also find people who bravely fight against oppression, bring salve to wounds, and rush to assist at any natural disaster. We have heard of people who find miraculous courage to rescue others from accidents. Allah ﷻ Who created us and gave us the choice, created the breeding ground for these great works.

Allah knows exactly who is helping. He knows who is giving. He knows who is bravely reaching out to support and carry.

Do not despair at the pain; rather rejoice at the beauty and blessings.

As the Abyssinian slave threw up his hands in confidence, let us also throw up our hands in confident *duʿāʾ*, calling on Allah ﷻ to send us rain. Let the rain fall upon our parched hearts and heal us all – all seven billion of us. *Āmīn*.

Reflection

Have you ever experienced the feeling of a *duʿāʾ* being answered? Do you find it easy to communicate with Allah through *duʿāʾ*? If it does not come easily for you, what do you think might be holding you back from deep, sincere prayers?

Project

Make a list of ten things you would like to make *duʿāʾ* for. Use your list to prompt you as you make *duʿāʾ* this week, for ten minutes each day. (Did you find yourself making *duʿāʾ* for more than the ten things on your list?)

Tip

Making your *duʿāʾ* out loud sometimes helps you find your flow and feel the depth of your requests. Try it!

Reflection / Project

_____
_____
_____
_____
_____
_____
_____
_____
_____
_____
_____
_____
_____
_____
_____
_____
_____
_____
_____
_____
_____
_____
_____

Week 9

Grievances, Grudges and the Spiritual Standstill

HOW MANY GRUDGES DO you carry in your heart?

Are those grudges helping you on your spiritual path?

In a series of instructions to believers, Allah ﷻ says in Sūrat Āl ʿImrān:

ٱلَّذِينَ يُنفِقُونَ فِى ٱلسَّرَّآءِ وَٱلضَّرَّآءِ وَٱلْكَٰظِمِينَ ٱلْغَيْظَ وَٱلْعَافِينَ عَنِ ٱلنَّاسِ وَٱللَّهُ يُحِبُّ ٱلْمُحْسِنِينَ ﴿١٣٤﴾

Who spend during ease and hardship and who restrain anger and who pardon the people – and Allah loves the doers of good. (3:134)

We are not to be people of bitter hearts, but rather forgiving hearts that pardon the shortcomings and perceived wrongdoings of people.

The Prophet ﷺ was hurt on a personal level when his Uncle Ḥamza ؓ was killed and mutilated. Hind bint ʿUtba was behind his murder, for he was not killed in the ordinary course of battle, but by the well-placed spear of an assassin, who had been hired to commit the act in return for his freedom. Ḥamza's ⚘ corpse was mutilated and Hind came forth and attempted to eat his liver. It was pure maliciousness. Yet when she came to the Prophet ﷺ after Fatḥ Mecca as a new convert to Islam, he accepted her with grace and forgiveness. He answered her questions and gave her personal advice about her marriage. Here is a crime that one could hold a grudge about – or so it would seem – yet our Prophet ﷺ was not a man of grudges. He forgave, he cared, he accepted.

What of those of us today who hold grudges because we were not invited to a wedding in a timely manner? Or because someone said something cold and hurtful to us?

Abū Bakr ⚘ used to give money to a relative of his who was poverty stricken. When the gossip and shameful slander of his daughter ʿĀʾisha ⚘ occurred, and once it was resolved, he swore never to give him money again because of his involvement. Allah the Exalted sent down a verse of the Quran admonishing Abū Bakr ⚘ for this grudge-bearing behavior:

وَلَا يَأْتَلِ أُوْلُواْ ٱلْفَضْلِ مِنكُمْ وَٱلسَّعَةِ أَن يُؤْتُوٓاْ أُوْلِي ٱلْقُرْبَىٰ وَٱلْمَسَٰكِينَ وَٱلْمُهَٰجِرِينَ فِي سَبِيلِ ٱللَّهِ وَلْيَعْفُواْ وَلْيَصْفَحُوٓاْ أَلَا تُحِبُّونَ أَن يَغْفِرَ ٱللَّهُ لَكُمْ وَٱللَّهُ غَفُورٌ رَّحِيمٌ ۝

And let not those of virtue among you and wealth swear not to give [aid] to their relatives and the needy and the emigrants for the cause of Allah, and let them pardon and overlook. Would you not like that Allah should forgive you? And Allah is Forgiving and Merciful. (24:22)

Holding a grudge and – even worse – acting upon it, are dangers in the path of our own forgiveness.

And indeed, once a grudge begins, it tends to hold on tight, squeezing empathy, kindness, compassion, and other qualities of a believer from the heart.

A Quality of Iblīs

Iblīs is the king of grudge holders (may we be protected from Shaiṭān). He resented our status with Allah ﷻ and refused to bow before us. When Allah ﷻ questioned him, he did not seek forgiveness and attempt to rectify his mistake, but instead, he let the bitter burning of resentment build within. His only request was to take us down with him.

Are we being dragged down the bitterness road? Have we begun to imitate Shaiṭān instead of the Prophet ﷺ?

We seek refuge from the cursed Shaiṭān, let us not take on his qualities. Wash your grudges from your hearts. Refuse to be bitter. Choose joy. Choose forgiveness. Choose faith.

Reflection

Read the project first this week.

What happened in your own heart when you made *duʿāʾ* for those you were hard-hearted toward? Did you feel any differently? What happened when you gave your gift?

Project

Last week we made *duʿāʾ* for things and people in our lives. This week, continue to make sincere *duʿāʾ* a part of your daily routine and take it one step further, making *duʿāʾ* for a person or people toward whom you have been holding bitter feelings. It could be a Muslim or a non-

Muslim, an old hurt or a current one, it can be the same person all week or you can choose a new person every day. Make *duʿāʾ* for their guidance, their well-being, their *dunyā* and their *ākhira*. Ask Allah to resolve the problem between you and replace hurt feelings with love (both by healing your heart and by guiding them to avoid hurtful actions). Then, at the end of the week, choose at least one of the people on your list and give them a gift, for the Prophet ﷺ told us, "Give gifts, for gifts take away malice." (*Musnad al-Imām Aḥmad*)

«تهادوا فإن الهدية تذهب وغر الصدر.»

Reflection / Project

_____

_____

_____

_____

_____

_____

_____

_____

_____

_____

_____

_____

_____

_____

_____

_____

_____

_____

_____

_____

_____

_____

Week 10

Birth

A T 5:47 AM ON July 7th – as the sun was rising – my niece Melody was born. She came into the world after twelve hours of painful labor – a few hours of less painful waiting (because of the epidural and the new 'laboring down', which I hadn't heard of until my sister was doing it) – and a couple hours of intense pushing. Then, miracle of miracles – there she was. A baby!

Birth explodes in the glory of God.

I said to my sister, "I do believe that atheists have never witnessed childbirth."

I marvel at the accessibility of this miracle. It happens all around us. It happens daily. It happens to people we know and people we do not know. In every corner of the globe – babies are born. And the process has not changed since the time of the Prophet ﷺ – certainly the availability of drugs and medical interventions when something goes wrong have saved many a baby's life and many a mom's life – but the essence of the process remains the same:

A woman is pregnant. At first she is not sure – but she suspects. Then the baby grows inside her. She suffers: has to go to the bathroom more often, might be in a constant state of nausea, her sense of smell changes, her body grows.

By the third trimester she is heavier than she has ever been in her life, she is hot in the coldest room, and she is uncomfortable in every position.

Then the pain comes. She knows something great is at the end of this pain, but she starts to wonder if it is worth it. She might swear at her husband and tell him that he will never touch her again! Or yell out that she cannot do it. Or just go quietly and deeply inside herself where she finds the strength to endure.

With the modern epidural, many women do not experience the intensity of that pain, but they still feel the contractions – they know they are there and they still remind them that something important is happening here.

Then the pushing begins. Strength and determination are needed to push out a baby. A woman has to aim right and push with all her might. No one can help her except as a cheering section. "Good job!" "Great one!" "Excellent!" But she is pushing alone.

Finally, the baby. First head, then shoulders, then the whole body comes slippery sliding out. *Subḥān Allah*! A baby! And no one can believe it. It is a moment of angels and miracles, a moment of truth and beauty, a moment when the glory of God is manifest before everyone's eyes. *Allāhu Akbar*.

It is a metaphor for every beginning, everything new in our lives. The 'new' grows; we change; we suffer... We might find an anesthetic to help, but the reality of the new remains. And then finally we must push. There may be people to cheer us on, but we will push alone. Finally, the 'new' will come slippery sliding out and we will glorify God; we will sing His praises, because what was so difficult is so worth it. *Allāhu Akbar*.

Reflection

Although some spiritual growth is an instantaneous miracle – a gift from Allah – most of the time it is more of a miraculous *process* that, especially at the beginning, takes time, effort and a lot of pushing ourselves to new levels. We must establish new habits that at first may cause us to suffer (getting up at night, disciplining our prayers, wrangling our unruly *nafs*...), but that will lead us to new heights of peace, tranquility and joy – as states of being, not just transient emotions.

Think of a time when you experienced a moment of growth. Remember what led up to it and what part of it caused you the most struggle and frustration. Now that you have set yourself on a new path of growth, how can you plan ahead to anticipate its challenges and obstacles, and help ensure that you will overcome them?

Project

Identify the challenges you are currently experiencing in one specific area of growth. Sit down and strategize ways you can overcome them. Think outside the box! Training your nafs is like training an athlete or even a puppy. You have to take practical steps to ease your path to success and offer rewards and consequences along the way. If your challenge is praying on time, perhaps you could set a goal of praying within 30 minutes of the *adhān*. Make sure you have an *adhān* alarm set up on your phone or computer, then reward yourself with a slice of pie or a new phone app if you manage to do it for three days running. If you miss it twice in one day, on the other hand, you could forbid yourself any social media or another form of entertainment the next day. Set out your plan here.

Goal

Plan

Rewards for accomplishments:

Consequences for missing the mark:

Reflection / Project

Week 11

The Mawlid

HE EARTH HELD NO prophet. Its people were lost in an utter darkness – no prophet, no current message, no light. The last prophet had lived and left the Earth hundreds of years before. There was an utter deprivation of righteousness. There was a hunger and a yearning for the return of the Divine Will – for the presence of one who would reflect that light.

A Jewish man ran through the streets of Mecca asking, "Was anyone born to you on this night?" None were sure and he cried out to them, "Find out, for on this night a prophet was born."

The midwife saw the stars come so near that she felt they would touch her, and at his ﷺ birth she saw nothing but light.

His mother saw a light emanating from her that lit the palaces of Shām – such that she could see them.

This child was the answer to Ibrāhīm's prayer and the good news of ʿĪsā.

The child was an end to the pause. The period of darkness, the prophet-less age, had come to an end. The final prophet was here. Never again would there be a pause in the Divine Will, or light – for Muhammad ﷺ was sent to all people, to all nations, to all generations till the end of time.

It happened on a Monday, the 12th of Rabīʿ al-Awwal, in the Year of the Elephant. The Prophet ﷺ was born. *Al-ḥamdu l-i-Llāh!* Our prophet! Born! What a day! A day for celebrations, thanksgiving! A day for happiness and smiles, congratulatory handshakes, and joyful kisses on the cheek, a day to be remembered.

The month of the Prophet's birth is a month of great joy for Muslims everywhere. And for centuries different cultures and peoples have recited poetry, gathered together and increased their good deeds in celebration and remembrance of his birth.

All Muslims agree that it is important to love the Prophet ﷺ, and that it is important to demonstrate that love in some way. There is a disagreement about whether or not celebrating his birth is an acceptable practice. This question is not a new one; many early scholars responded to it and as such, the practice has become widespread amongst Muslims. In every country there are special songs, traditional foods, and a moving poem that venerates our beloved Messenger.

Some of the early scholars, who responded to the question, "Mawlid?" include:

- Imām al-Sakhāwī, who said, "In every land and every city, the Islamic people continue to celebrate his ﷺ birth by holding fine gatherings involving all manner of dignified celebration, making many charitable donations by night, expressing their joy, increasing their righteous acts, and reading the story of his glorious birth, and thus the all-embracing grace of this blessed time is manifest in them."

- Al-Suyūṭī, who quoted Ibn Ḥajar as giving the example of the day of ʿĀshūrāʾ– that Prophet Muhammad ﷺ called upon Muslims to fast this day in celebration of the victory of Moses over Pharaoh, thus it is valid to celebrate days of blessing. Al-Suyūṭī then comments, "What blessing is greater than the birth of the Prophet, the Prophet of Mercy, on this day?"

- Imām Ibn al-Jawzī says about the celebrated Mawlid, "It is security throughout the year, and glad tidings that all wishes and desires will be fulfilled." After all, the Prophet fulfilled the most important desire and yearning of the heart for us all, he taught us how to reach God.

The month of the Prophet's birth 🌺 is a celebration: a celebration of the blessing of a living, breathing example of how Allah 🌺 wants us to live, a celebration of the birth of the final Prophet, a celebration of the greatest blessing the earth was ever to receive.

Let us bring joy into our homes in recognition of his birth. We can begin yearly traditions that build attachment to his person and his teachings. An annual re-reading of the *sīra*, an evening of singing songs about him or cooking and eating some of his favorite foods are some possible ways to celebrate.

Our religion, our serenity, our strength: it all began with this man, on the day of his birth. *Allāhu Akbar* and *Al-hamdu l-i-Llāh*. What a joyous day, a joyous month, a joyous season. *Allāhumma ṣalli ʿalā sayyidinā wa habībinā* Muhammad. O God, send peace and blessings upon our master and our beloved Muhammad.

Reflection

Reflect for a moment about how we celebrate each other. We celebrate important people and events in our lives with dinners, parties, and gifts. We applaud accomplishments and cheer for good effort. How, then, might we celebrate our beloved Prophet 🌺?

Project

Make a goal of bringing the Prophet and praise of him into your life this week. One of the best ways to bring love of the Prophet  into your heart is to make *ṣalawāt*. Say "*Allāhumma ṣalli ʿalā sayyidinā Muhammad*" 100 times after each prayer and watch how your heart softens! Make sure to talk about the Prophet ﷺ – his love for us and his superb character, his achievements and his mercy – with your family and friends so they begin to know him and love him as well.

Reflection / Project

_____

_____

_____

_____

_____

_____

_____

_____

_____

_____

_____

_____

_____

_____

_____

_____

_____

_____

_____

Week 12

Ebullient Emulation

OUR PROPHET ﷺ WAS A unique individual. His orphaned state made him sensitive to the needs of others, his poverty made him creative in problem solving, his heritage gave him every thread of beauty and strength as well as the love and honor of his people, and Allah ﷻ sent him people to fill in the gaps of a missing father, mother, and grandfather. Through all of this he earned the names "the trustworthy", "the honest" and "the dependable". This was before he received the revelation.

In order to carry the message, Allah prepared the Prophet ﷺ and protected him. He manifested this in his life and deeds – in his very being.

In order for us to carry on the responsibility of this message, to inherit the work of the Prophet ﷺ, we must be prepared and protected. We must manifest our preparedness in our lives and deeds and beings.

In the last ten days of Rabīʿ al-Awwal, let us celebrate his birth in our very being.

1. Let us send 1000 ṣalawāt each day.

   Allah and His angels send blessings on the Prophet: O you that believe! Send your blessings on him, and salute him with all respect. (33:56)

إِنَّ ٱللَّهَ وَمَلَـٰئِكَتَهُۥ يُصَلُّونَ عَلَى ٱلنَّبِىِّ يَـٰٓأَيُّهَا ٱلَّذِينَ ءَامَنُوا۟ صَلُّوا۟ عَلَيْهِ وَسَلِّمُوا۟ تَسْلِيمًا ۝

The Prophet ﷺ said, "Whoever sends one prayer upon me, God sends ten prayers upon him and records for him ten good deeds." (*Sunan al-Tirmidhī*)

«مَنْ صَلَّى عَلَيَّ صَلاةً صَلَّى اللهُ عَلَيهِ عَشْراً وَكُتِبَ لَهُ عَشْرُ حَسَناتٍ.»

He also said, "None sends greetings of peace upon me, but that God returns my soul so that I may return to him the greeting of peace." (*Sunan Abī Dāwūd*)

«ما من أحدٍ يسلم عليَّ إلاَّ ردَّ اللهُ عليَّ روحي حتَّى أردَّ عليه السلام.»

Sending peace and blessings upon the Prophet is a deeply embedded practice of Muslims. It helps to develop a relationship between us, and draws us near to his being. We are encouraged to do it as much as possible, and there is no set number that must be done, or a number that is too few. To set a goal of one thousand per day is to set our mind upon developing that relationship and celebrating his life and his message. May Allah make us of those who truly love the Prophet ﷺ!

2. Let us connect the ties of kin and call family members we have not talked to for a while.

Abū Ayyūb al-Anṣārī tells us that a bedouin came to the Prophet, may Allah bless him and grant him peace, while he was travelling. He asked, "Tell me what will bring me near to the Garden and keep me far from the Fire." He ﷺ replied, "Worship Allah and do

60

not associate anything with Him, perform the prayer, pay zakat, and maintain ties of kinship." (*Ṣaḥīḥ al-Bukhārī*)

«تعبد الله ولا تشرك به شيئا، وتقيم الصلاة،

وتؤتي الزكاة، وتصل الرحم.»

The Prophet ﷺ was known to be a person who kept his family together. When he returned to Khadīja ؓ afraid and unsure of what had just occurred, saying, "I fear for myself," she replied, "No, by God, God would never humiliate you. Verily, you remain in touch with your kin, help the burdened, give to the impoverished, honor your guest and assist in any upright cause."

As we hold on to our familial relationships, our relationship with the Prophet will develop. As we honor and respect the elders in our family and deal gently and lovingly with the children, we will grow in faith. The Prophetic character showed in his interactions with people. Our families deserve and have a right to our best character. Let us honor him ﷺ by reconnecting with our family, gathering them together, and standing as the cement pillar that holds them up.

3. Let us wake up at night and pray *tahajjud*.

And rise from sleep during the night – it is an additional prayer for you. Perhaps your Lord will raise you to an honored position. (17:79)

وَمِنَ ٱلَّيْلِ فَتَهَجَّدْ بِهِۦ نَافِلَةً لَّكَ

عَسَىٰٓ أَن يَبْعَثَكَ رَبُّكَ مَقَامًا مَّحْمُودًا ۝

The lifestyle of the companions included *tahajjud*. It is said amongst the people of God, "One does not become a person of God except through the nightly prayer, or Ramadan."

If we are to withstand the onslaught of distractions and blatant sin, we must, as individuals and as a community, become people of *tahajjud*. It is our only real hope in overcoming the state we find ourselves in.

Two *rakʿas* at night, fifteen minutes before Fajr, is an excellent beginning. Let us celebrate the Prophet and emulate him in bringing life and light to our nights.

Three new habits, sending *ṣalawāt*, pulling our families together, and praying *tahajjud*, will set us firmly on the path of love. We will begin to emulate this unique man, our Prophet ﷺ, our beloved and His beloved, and find ourselves in the shade of his character. As we draw strength, we will begin to inherit the work of the Messengers, and the message of *tawḥīd* will find itself gaining strength on the Earth once again.

Peace and blessings be upon him.

Reflection

If there is a barrier between you and your family, what put it there? What can you do to chip away at it? If there is no barrier, what can you do to take your relationship with them to the next level and truly show them the character of the Prophet ﷺ?

Project

Reach out to a member of your family in some way *this very week*. If there is animosity or distance between you and one specific family member, begin the process of curing it and drawing closer. Make a call, send a note or drop an email. Give a gift, ask forgiveness or grant it in your heart. And keep it up weekly from here on out.

Reflection / Project

Week 13

The Yearly Spreadsheet

EVERY HUMAN BEING IS allotted the same number of hours each week.

Sometimes I imagine these hours spread out on yearly spreadsheets – where every hour has a detailed account of how it was spent: the words we said, the attitudes we had, the moments we remembered Allah ﷻ. It is a formidable image.

Sometimes I meet people who complain a lot about having 'no time'. They constantly jabber on and on about how they can't do this or they can't do that because they just 'don't have time.' Then I meet other people who are drenched in both responsibilities and accomplishments. Yet we all have the same 24 hours... right?

Time, while it is equitably distributed, is a malleable force.

In a hadith *qudsi* it is said, "Allah said, 'The son of Adam wrongs me for he curses *al-dahr* (Time), though I am Al-Dahr (Time). In My Hands are all things, and I cause the revolution of day and night.'" (*Ṣaḥīḥ al-Bukhārī*).

«قال الله عز وجل: يؤذيني ابن آدم، يسب الدهر وأنا الدهر، بيدي الأمر، أقلب الليل والنهار.»

There are physical rules that Allah ﷻ has set forth for

this earth: gravity makes us fall, fire burns us, ice freezes us, for example. And we all have to follow these rules – Allah is All-Powerful and can make exceptions to the rules (such as when he commanded the fire to be cool for Ibrāhīm, for example) but for the most part we will all burn our fingers if we hold them next to a flame. Allah ﷻ also controls time, yet our Prophet ﷺ said, "Take advantage of five matters before five other matters: your youth before you become old, your health before you fall sick, your wealth before you become poor, your free time before you become preoccupied, and your life before your death." (Narrated by Ibn ʿAbbās in the *Mustadrak of al-Ḥākim and Musnad al-Imām Aḥmad*)

»اغتنم خمسا قبل خمس: شبابك قبل هرمك،
وصحتك قبل سقمك ، وغناك قبل فقرك،
وفراغك قبل شغلك، وحياتك قبل موتك.«

Just as we learn to interact with Allah's earthly rules (don't walk off a cliff, make sure to wear your winter coat), we must learn to interact with His rules of time. We must take advantage of our free time, we must plan our busy time. We must always know that time is in the hands of God, and it is He who gives it blessing or takes the blessing away.

Teachers of time management courses all agree that those who set a goal, prepare a plan, work hard and have a positive attitude are most likely to succeed. They will also find time the most malleable.

Indeed, living in the way of the Prophet ﷺ – worshipping at night and being diligent during the day – is the key to hours that stretch to hold much goodness.

- What is your goal? We all wish for the pleasure of Allah and His *janna*. But what does that mean to you in manageable chunks?

- How do you plan to reach that goal? Our *nafs* is so well nourished that many of us no longer see it as something that must be tamed, but rather as something that must be satiated. Lofty goals need hard work. Are we willing to sacrifice our comfort for spiritual success? *Da'wa* success? Or only for worldly success? Many a Muslim will sacrifice years and years, go into great debt and give up sleep and social engagements in order to earn a degree. Yet how many of those same Muslims will put equal effort into memorizing the Quran? Every goal needs a plan.

- How hard are you willing to work? And are you willing to work without a 'thank-you' in this life? Many people are willing to work 'for Allah', but when they feel 'mistreated' or 'unappreciated', they flip their heads around and haughtily walk the other way, all the while exclaiming, "I tried!" or "No good deed goes unpunished by the people!" We must be willing to work and struggle for Allah and His religion. He says:

Say, "If your fathers, your sons, your brothers, your wives, your relatives, wealth which you have obtained, commerce wherein you fear decline, and dwellings with which you are pleased are more beloved to you than Allah and His Messenger and jihad in His cause, then wait until Allah executes His command. And Allah does not guide the defiantly disobedient people." (9:24)

قُلْ إِن كَانَ ءَابَآؤُكُمْ وَأَبْنَآؤُكُمْ وَإِخْوَٰنُكُمْ وَأَزْوَٰجُكُمْ وَعَشِيرَتُكُمْ وَأَمْوَٰلٌ ٱقْتَرَفْتُمُوهَا وَتِجَٰرَةٌ تَخْشَوْنَ كَسَادَهَا وَمَسَٰكِنُ تَرْضَوْنَهَآ أَحَبَّ إِلَيْكُم مِّنَ

$$\text{ٱللَّهِ وَرَسُولِهِۦ وَجِهَادٍ فِى سَبِيلِهِۦ فَتَرَبَّصُواْ حَتَّىٰ يَأْتِىَ ٱللَّهُ بِأَمْرِهِۦ ۗ وَٱللَّهُ لَا يَهْدِى ٱلْقَوْمَ ٱلْفَٰسِقِينَ ۝}$$

This is a truly powerful verse. We must love Allah, His messenger and *working in His cause* more than our very selves and all the trappings of this *dunyā*. If we truly love Him, when work in His cause truly becomes important, we will work hard and have no need of human appreciation.

• Can you manufacture a positive attitude? Shaikh Bashīr al-Bānī (may Allah have mercy on his soul) wrote a book entitled, "The Prophet ﷺ was a 'Yes,'" and the entire book is example after example of how positive and optimistic he ﷺ was. Can we embody that? Even when things look bleak? Can we have that deep *riḍā* (contentment)? For Allah? The Prophet's optimism was seen in his interactions with people and in his daily life. In the struggles of Mecca, he was patient with garbage found at his doorstep every day. On the day it was not there, he asked about the woman who had been putting it there, in concern for her health. He invited his entire family for dinner, fed them, and when he was about to speak, Abū Lahab interrupted and the opportunity was lost. He invited them again, fed them again, and this time spoke immediately. He wasn't deterred or depressed by his uncle's negativity. At al-Ṭāʾif, after being chased out of the town, his *duʿāʾ* was, "As long as You are not angry with me, then all is well." (*Kanz al-ʿUmmāl*).

$$\text{«إن لم تكن ساخطا علي فلا أبالي.»}$$

His optimism is almost unfathomable. Again and again throughout his life, he interacted with situations and people positively and optimistically. If we are to take advantage of our time, we must embody this quality of the Prophet 繁. Negativity is a time thief and we are 'too busy' for that!

On the Day of Judgment we will be raised with the people who came before us and the people who came after us. All of us will be held to account for the same 24 hours in our days. Let us be of those who are not embarrassed by our spreadsheets. *Āmīn*.

Reflection

Sit down and take stock of how you are spending your time. How much time do you think you are spending in productive activities and how much would you say you are wasting? Are there things you would like to be able to do or accomplish but you do not have time for? Write them here.

Project

Make seven copies of the Daily Plan provided on the next page. For the first three days, write down your activities *every half hour* during your waking moments, and track your sleep as well. Then total up how much time you are using productively and how much you are wasting. Pay particular attention to "empty hours." Then plan out the next four days, and stick to that schedule. Did you surprise yourself? Did you get more done than usual? Go back now and look at those activities you said you'd like to have time for. Do you feel more able to confidently schedule them in now?

Tip

Remember to keep up the habits you form from this exercise. Be wary of black holes such as social media, video games, television, etc.

Reflection / Project

Daily Plan

0:00		8:00		16:00	
0:30		8:30		16:30	
1:00		9:00		17:00	
1:30		9:30		17:30	
2:00		10:00		18:00	
2:30		10:30		18:30	
3:00		11:00		19:00	
3:30		11:30		19:30	
4:00		12:00		20:00	
4:30		12:30		20:30	
5:00		13:00		21:00	
5:30		13:30		21:30	
6:00		14:00		22:00	
6:30		14:30		22:30	
7:00		15:00		23:00	
7:30		15:30		23:30	

Week 14

There is Enough

E LIVE IN AN age of fear.

We are afraid of what people will say, afraid of what the weather might be tomorrow, and afraid of how the economy might go next year.

We are afraid to eat the chocolate cake, afraid to step on the scale and afraid to call an old friend.

We are afraid to watch the news, afraid to discipline our children and afraid to eat a grocery store tomato.

Islam comes as a cure for the rumbling fear. It tells us to trust, rely and depend on our Lord. The Prophet (peace and blessings be upon him) taught Abū Huraira 🕮 this lesson when he 🕮 found him hungry and invited him to his home for a bowl of milk.

Abū Huraira was extremely hungry. We know that people who live in a state of want can become anxious, depressed and even violent. Maslow teaches us that one of the basic needs of the human being is food. Certainly all the dieting folk around the world prove that food influences our moods, as they growl and groan at their loved ones while staying under 1200 calories a day.

A person who stays for a long period of time without enough food may begin to fear for his strength, his health and even his life.

When the Prophet ﷺ invited Abū Huraira ؓ to his home for a bowl of milk, Abū Huraira had already been hungry for a long time. He was ravenous. After he saw the milk, the Prophet ﷺ instructed him to go and get the others who lived in the mosque, who were more than likely also hungry. Abū Huraira recounts that this made him upset, because he felt he had the most right to that milk (he was afraid, perhaps, that there would not be enough), but since he could not disobey the Messenger of God, he went forth and retrieved them all.

Once they returned, the Prophet ﷺ gave the bowl to Abū Huraira and instructed him to give it to the others first. *Subḥān Allah.* Abū Huraira was first! He was so very hungry. Yet the Prophet was a teacher and guide of humanity, and Abū Huraira had something to learn.

After every one of them had drunk from the bowl, and only the Prophet and Abū Huraira remained, Prophet Muhammad ﷺ asked Abū Huraira to sit and drink his fill. He did. When he was finished, he gave the bowl over to the Prophet ﷺ, who finished it off.

There was enough.

And whenever we are afraid, we must remember that. There is enough. There is enough food to go around, enough love and enough joy.

Fear is a tool of Shaiṭān. It steals our faith and turns us into mean and disagreeable people.

When we rid ourselves of fear and trust in Allah ﷻ, we hang on to the rope of faith and become kind, generous and empathetic people.

May we be of those willing to serve the bowl of milk before partaking of it ourselves. May we be of those who throw fear out the window and replace it with *taqwā* (awareness of God) and *tawakkul* (trust in God). *Āmīn.*

Reflection

What are you afraid of? What is holding you back from being as giving, as loving, as relaxed or as productive as you could be? Where did it come from and why do you think you have not been able to overcome it?

Project

Is fear of not having enough sustenance holding you back in your personal, spiritual or professional life? Sometimes we fear not having the emotional wherewithal to help someone else; sometimes we fear not having enough time and so avoid committing to important projects; sometimes we fear not having enough money so we hold back from giving charity. Of course, when this happens, our growth is stunted. Sit down each day this week and make *du'ā'* about your fears for ten minutes. In this way you are acknowledging your fears to Allah and putting your trust in Him that He will help you grow past them and provide you with more than enough sustenance to offer and do and give all that you should.

Reflection / Project

Week 15

Mosqued

The unmosqueing, demosqueing, remosqueing, bemosquing and nothankyoumosqueing of our communities.

In my early days of Islam I was shocked and horrified by my mosque experiences. I felt humiliated, isolated, oppressed, dejected and rejected. I never spoke about these experiences, never told anyone how I felt being relegated to a little room with filthy dirty carpet and screaming babies, while the few men spread out on pristine oriental carpets in the quiet and sacrosanct men's area. I never mentioned how it felt to have someone call me a '*kāfir*' and organize an intervention for me because I had stopped wearing one style of hijab and opted for another. I never shared the frightening comparisons happening in my head as I realized I had never, ever been treated like this in a church. I never spoke about any of it, not even to myself.

Instead, I walked away. I turned to Islamic scholarship, seeking comfort in the practices of Prophet Muhammad ﷺ, and spent many years healing my torn soul.

I believed myself stronger when I returned to the United States and to the American Muslim community after twenty years abroad. But I wasn't.

I found myself in a tiny balcony with a large city ordinance posted at one end, warning that the balcony could safely hold no more than twenty people. I kept counting the women and children and praying the balcony would not collapse.

I tried another mosque, but my smiles and *salāms* were to no avail as I was nodded at and skirted around. I went back anyway because the women's section had been clean and I could both see and hear the imam. When I returned, though, a rough and messy curtain had been placed between the women and the men. I prayed and went home.

At four other mosques I offered to teach (Quran, Islamic sciences, children, adults), and showed them that I spoke Arabic, have an *ijāza* in Quran, and had studied sacred knowledge for over twenty years. I was politely turned away.

In essence the unmosqueing of my youth became the demosqueing of my adulthood.

It is time to start talking about this. It is time to raise respectful voices. It is time for women to find a welcome mat at the door of any mosque they happen to visit.

There are a number of possible solutions to the problems in our mosques today. More than likely a combination of all of them will bring us to the best conclusion.

1. Create third spaces. A third space that is not charged with the "sacredness" of mosque space offers a safe place for people to meet and talk about religious matters. It can be a 'come as you are to become as you wish you were' type of place.

2. Identify the simple problems and be the solution. I see one of our greatest failures in the mosque as our failure to welcome people to it. I recently attended a Friday prayer that was almost revolutionary. After the prayer, the imam casually walked around, joining groups of people and asking who was new so that he could welcome them. He made his way to the

women's section, and gave his *salāms*, asking about the new women who were there. By chance there was a guest from out of town, a woman getting her PhD in education; they exchanged cards when they discovered that their research interests had some overlap. Everyone felt welcome and important. It reminded me of how the companions felt around the Messenger ﷺ. Of course it does not have to be the imam who greets people after the prayer; mosques can have someone standing at the door – giving *salāms* and finding the new people, helping them find their way to the shoe area, the *wudū'* area and the prayer area. This little change will make a significant difference in the accessibility of our mosques.

3. Become policy makers. We must be appreciative of the hard work that mosque boards put into the mosque. If we want to criticize, we must be willing to join hands and put in hours of work to affect the changes we envision. In attempting to create change, it is helpful to look at research about change, to remember that change is difficult for most people, and to be very patient and gentle in our approach.

Women must take the initiative to make spaces wherein we can live in the shelter of each other. We have a generation to raise, a generation that needs to be connected to sacred spaces if they are to be able to grow and deepen their own spiritual selves. It is of primary importance that we begin to address the issue of the mosque as a place of prayer and a place of community. May we bring back the tradition of our beloved Prophet and find solace in our sacred spaces. *Āmīn*.

Reflection

Is your mosque the healthy, welcoming, clean place you wish it were? If not, write here about the top three issues you'd like to improve in order to bring it closer to the Prophetic ideal.

Project

Choose at least one of the issues you wrote above and set about addressing it! By founding a third space, by volunteering for a role you feel needs to be filled, by submitting feedback to the suggestion box, by cleaning the prayer room, by running for office, or simply by opening your own heart. Make a point to greet five – yes FIVE – people you do not know the next time you go to your mosque. Hug them, smile at them, ask about them! Start mosqueing each other! Be the change you wish to see in the mosque.

Reflection / Project

Week 16

Revert or Convert?

*L*ABELING TELLS US WHO we really are – and we describe ourselves in many ways. I am an American. I am a teacher. I am female. I am a student. I am a reader. I am a coffee-drinker. Sometimes we label ourselves, and other times we are labeled by others. As a person who was not born into Islam, I have been labeled with many names – crazy, Arab wannabe, towelhead. None of these labels imposed upon me by others has ever had a particular effect on me, yet the twenty-year-old habit of calling me (and those like me) a 'revert' has given me pause.

At some point over twenty years ago, someone latched on to the idea that we are all born upon *fitra* – or with an inherent tendency toward *tawhīd* – and thus the term 'revert' was born. It was meant to indicate that those who had newly entered Islam had actually returned to their original state of being.

I, for one, have never felt comfortable with the label 'revert'. I do not like being corrected by others when I introduce myself as a convert, nor do I appreciate being introduced as a revert, with a proverbial pat on my head, to other Muslims. The word 'revert' has the semantic implication of going backwards. It can be used instead of the word 'relapse' or 'regress'. The Arabic translation of the word would be *murtadd*, a horrible word meaning one that has turned back and away from their religion. The word convert, on the other hand, implies change. It can be used to talk about electricity charges, home renovations, and spiritual transformations.

Somehow we have been bullied into using the word 'revert'. The first time I heard it I was interrupted. I had been introducing myself, "I'm a convert," I said. "No, you are a revert," I was told. It sat upon my heart – but I was young and impressionable – so I assumed (as most good converts do) that the Arabic-speaking and Arabic-last-name-having person in front of me was 'right'. But I am older now, and less impressionable, and no longer willing to be bullied into a vocabulary that I find unbefitting to the conversion process.

Becoming a Muslim is an arduous affair. There are layers and layers involved in the process. A new Muslim has already changed her belief system. She must think about Jesus in a new way (if she was a Christian), and get to know Muhammad ﷺ. The book she will now read for guidance and light needs a new language for full access, and – while she may always have believed in God as One – she now has a new name to get used to (Allah).

A new Muslim must change her habits. She will begin to pray in a certain way – and in order to do so must memorize words and phrases that will, for a time, carry little meaning. She will change what she eats, and how she eats it. She may have to drop friends, perhaps the boyfriend that introduced her to Islam. She will have to deal with many people telling her what is 'right' and what is 'wrong' – often with contradictory opinions. She may hear erroneous claims that challenge her fledgling belief, and she may get frustrated with her new 'friends' and their strangeness.

When I became a Muslim, I lived with some young Malaysian students. They were a great blessing in my life – I loved them. They taught me things one could never read in a book. I remember one day one of my new friends, Jamaatun, asked me why I had not prayed Witr. I had never heard of the prayer, but she answered for herself saying, "Oh, I guess you will pray it with *tahajjud*," to which I nodded – though I didn't know what that was either. So she set me firmly on a path of worship. Yet I also remember feeling 'elephant-like' around my newfound Malaysian friends; they were so petite and gentle, while I was a loud and large American. While I appreciated their care and guidance and loved them dearly, I also had a sense of longing for someone who would understand why I wanted a piece of pie, for alas, I soon discovered that pie was a uniquely American dessert, and it would be years before I met another Muslim who ever had the thought, "I could really use a piece of pie right now."

Converts to Islam run the gamut of life transformation: I have known converts who entered into Islam yet remained in an illicit relationship, and I have known converts who entered into Islam and changed everything about themselves – even those things that did not need changing. Of course I have also known many converts in between those two extremes. The road that the convert enters upon is a lifelong path. She will face challenges as a neophyte and then face new challenges as a seasoned veteran of her faith. I suppose this is why the name she calls herself is important to me. Revert implies that it is finished – she has gone back to something and she is done with that. Convert implies what is truer about the path – a continuous transformation, a continuous revamping, rebuilding, and renewing of her faith.

She who has converted to Islam has indeed taken an important first step on the path to God, but there are many more steps that will follow that first one. In the label 'convert' is the cognizance of the choice she has made.

Reflection

Have you been in the habit of using either convert or revert? Do you have reasons for your preference? Have you felt pressured to use one or the other?

Project

Whether you are a convert yourself or are from a Muslim family, reach out to a convert in your community this week. Think about the layers of transformation she is uncovering and the lifelong process of growing in a new faith that she has embarked upon – perhaps without the support of her family. Think, as well, about the finger-wagging or cultural "teaching" she may be enduring at the hands of some. Ease her path this week! Take her out for coffee or dinner (just for fun!), offer to be her Fajr or *tahajjud* buddy, or make her a care package and deliver it to her door. Find a way to make her feel supported and cared for.

Reflection / Project

Week 17

Love is a Verb

Love is what turns bitter to sweet, dirt to gold, murkiness to clarity, pain to cure, prison to meadow, sickness to blessing and compulsion to mercy. It is that which softens iron, melts rock, resurrects the dead and turns slave into master. All patients wish for cure from their disease except the lovelorn, who ask for more and would like their pain and longing to be increased. No drink have I seen sweeter than this poison, and no health better than this illness. It is an illness that cures all illnesses, and those who contract it will never fall sick. It is the healthy state of the spirit, or the spirit of health. Those who live in bounty would exchange their wealth for it.

Jalāl al-Dīn al-Rūmī

THIS WEEK, ALL AROUND the world, people are either celebrating Valentine's Day or drowning in self-pity because they are not celebrating it. The stores are filled with heart-shaped chocolate boxes and ten-dollar gifts meant to empty consumers' pockets. Muslims on Facebook and in local mosques are debating and discussing the Muslim stance toward this holiday.

And everywhere we are missing the point.

Real love is love that elevates. It is not an obsession or

a passing fancy. It changes the spirit for the better. It is Divine love. This Divine love is what we mean when we say, "I love so-and-so for Allah's sake." This is a deep and important statement. It is standing in the shade of Allah's throne on the day upon which there is no other shade. It is tasting the sweetness of faith. It is living right.

Anas b. Mālik ﷺ tells us that the Prophet ﷺ said, "Whoever possesses these three things will find the sweetness of faith: That God and His Messenger are more beloved to him than anything other than them, that *he loves someone only for the sake of God*, and that he detests returning to disbelief as he detests being thrown into the fire." (*Ṣaḥīḥ Muslim and al-Bukhārī*)

«ثلاث من كن فيه وجد حلاوة الإيمان: أن يكون الله ورسوله أحب إليه مما سواهما، وأن يحب المرء لا يحبه إلا لله، وأن يكره أن يعود في الكفر كما يكره أن يقذف في النار.»

Love is a verb. In order to love someone for Allah's sake, we must love her with *taqwā*. We must put our *nafs* aside and be empathetic. We must love her as the companions loved each other.

'Umar ﷺ loved 'Ayyāsh and gave him money, property and a listening ear followed up with *duʿā'* and active care when 'Ayyāsh succumbed to the trial of Quraish.

Salmān al-Fārisī ﷺ loved Abū al-Dardā' and shared his experiences, while empathetically encouraging him to 'lighten up'.

Zainab bint Jaḥsh ﷺ loved 'Ā'isha ﷺ and responded when asked about her character, "She is purer than I," though it would have been to her advantage to say otherwise.

To love someone for Allah – to love a person as the companions loved each other – we must do the following:

1. Put our own personal benefit aside. Let us work on these hearts of ours.

2. Be willing to set aside our comfort zone. Let us be of those who care more for others than ourselves.

3. Give gifts, money, property, food and time. Let us be generous.

4. Pray for our beloved at night. Let us pray long and hard for those we love and those we do not love, that we may begin to love them.

5. Stop defending ourselves and start seeing the good in others (without the qualifying "but"). Let us seek to empathize with others and deeply understand their circumstances and feelings.

Love is a verb, and when we actively love someone – act in a way that is loving, even when we feel selfish, crabby, and spiteful – it becomes a feeling.

When we learn to imitate the companions and love each other truly and deeply, we will taste the sweetness of faith and our lives will become sweeter. That sweetness will spread throughout our families and communities, and our neighbors and co-workers will become curious. Love is a verb. Love.

Reflection

Often when we say we love someone, what we really mean is that they make us feel good. We mistakenly believe that love is a feeling rather than a deliberate action. This can result in the belief that we "no longer love" that person. Is there someone in your life with whom you have had this experience? Were you able to successfully transfer those initial, rather selfish feelings of "love" to real, selfless love?

Project

Dr. M. Scott Peck said, "Love is the will to extend one's self for the purpose of nurturing one's own or another's spiritual growth... Love is as love does." Choose a person whom you love and extend yourself for him/her this week. Go above and beyond all calls of duty, find ways to serve, make *duᶜā'*, and walk out of your comfort zone to be supportive. Concentrate on the fact that love means you want the best for them – rather than wanting to get the best from them. This exercise is even more important if you have been struggling to love them of late.

Reflection / Project

_____

_____

_____

_____

_____

_____

_____

_____

_____

_____

_____

_____

_____

_____

_____

_____

_____

_____

_____

_____

_____

_____

Week 18

Who We Are and
Who We Can Become:
The Story of Banī al-Azd

A DELEGATION OF SEVENTEEN MEN of Banī al-Azd came to the Prophet 🕊 in the ninth year after the *hijra*. It is said that the Prophet 🕊 was impressed with how they presented themselves before him and asked them, "Who are you?"

Banī al-Azd had already entered Islam at the hand of the emissary that the Messenger of God 🕊 had sent to them earlier in the year, so when the Prophet 🕊 asked them, "Who are you?" they responded, "Believers."

The Prophet 🕊 smiled and challenged them, "For everything said, there is proof; what is the proof of your belief?"

They responded that they had fifteen examples of their belief, five things the Prophet's emissary had instructed them to believe in, five things he had ordered them to do, and five things they brought forth from their lives before Islam.

The story of Banī al-Azd resonates with me, because so many come to Islam with beautiful and wonderful characteristics and qualities. They are honest, genuine and sincere. I have seen Muslims doubt these good qualities within themselves when overwhelmed with rules and unclear lines between culture and religion.

The Prophet ﷺ asked them about all fifteen examples, saying, when asking about the last five, "And what are the five upon which you were raised in *jāhiliyya*?"

They answered, "Gratefulness in times of plenty, forbearance in times of trial, contentedness in the face of bitter fate, courage in times of battle and the leaving of gloating over enemies."

The Prophet ﷺ responded with words of praise that are almost unbelievable in their beauty. He said, "Wise and learned, their depth of understanding brings them to [the level of] prophets."

His absolute approval of their good qualities is a loud and clear statement. We must always have open eyes to the truth around us. We must never deny the good and admirable within ourselves and our larger communities. Here the Prophet himself ﷺ praises and elevates the good qualities of a people – qualities that are presented as having originated in *jāhiliyya*. We learn that good is good. That Islam affirms goodness and rejects the bad and the ugly. In our hearts we know the difference. Wherever true goodness is found, we will recognize it as that which is beautiful and we will recognize it as part of faith, if we are people of wisdom and learning.

The Prophet ﷺ was always helping people be their best selves, and to the delegation of Banī al-Azd he said, "I shall increase your examples [of belief] by five more, such that they will be twenty." Here he assigned five difficult and ascetic human qualities: "If you are as you say you are, then do not collect what you will not eat, and do not build that which you will not live in, and do not compete over that which you will give up on the morrow, and have *taqwā* of God, to Whom you will return, and in front of

Whom you will be presented, and focus on that which is before you and is eternal." (*Al-Bidāya wa-l-Nihāya*)

»فلا تجمعوا مالا تأكلون، ولا تبنوا مالا تسكنون، ولا تنافسوا في شيء انتم عنه غدا تزولون، واتقوا الله الذي اليه ترجعون وعليه تعرضون، وارغبوا فيما عليه تقدمون وفيه تخلدون.«

It is said that Banī al-Azd held to the Prophet's 鬒 words and directives.

Are we as open to molding and improving our good qualities as Banī al-Azd? Our refrigerators often hold more than we will eat. We often desire more 'house' than we need. We compete over things like our weight and our possessions – all of which will matter little as we age. Our *taqwā* waxes and wanes depending on whose company we keep and the events of the day. And our focus is rarely on the *ākhira*, but rather on this very moment and matters of this *dunyā*. What about at the first moments of a meeting with the Prophet 鬒? Would he 鬒 be as impressed with us? Would the way we stand and speak demonstrate an inherent goodness? Would he ask us, "Who are you?" and would we be able to answer, "Believers," and be ready with proof?

Are we walking and breathing examples of good character? Are we wise and learned?

Are we ready to move further along the path of faith? Will it be said of us, "They followed the words and directives of the Prophet 鬒?"

Yā Rabb – may our answer become and always be: "Yes!"

Reflection

What are some of the good qualities you were raised with? What are some good qualities and characteristics you learned from non-Mulims?

What are your talents? Have you found ways to bring your talents forward and share them with the Muslim community?

Project

Choose one quality, talent or characteristic you have and write down ways you can focus that blessing on serving Allah and humanity.

Are you very organized? Organize meals for someone who is housebound.

Do you have performing talents? Consider starting a women's drama troupe or *nashīd* group. You might also work with Muslim youth or write a play.

Are you an animal lover? Consider teaching other Muslims how to care for animals or volunteer at a local animal shelter.

Make a commitment to bringing your whole self to Islam this week!

Reflection / Project

Week 19

Nafs Training

LLAH ﷻ SAYS IN Sūrat al-Nisā':

O you who believe, be upholders of justice, bearing witness to God – though it be against your own selves (nafs) *or your parents or kin....* (4:135)

۞ يَـٰٓأَيُّهَا ٱلَّذِينَ ءَامَنُوا۟ كُونُوا۟ قَوَّٰمِينَ بِٱلْقِسْطِ شُهَدَآءَ لِلَّهِ وَلَوْ عَلَىٰٓ أَنفُسِكُمْ أَوِ ٱلْوَٰلِدَيْنِ وَٱلْأَقْرَبِينَ

In this verse, Allah ﷻ calls upon us to stand against our '*nafs*' in our walk towards Him, and to help our parents and relatives in what is right (as opposed to helping them just because they are our relatives, or siding with them in something that is unjust or wrong).

Our *nafs* – loosely defined as that which calls us to fulfill our whims and desires – is recognizable in almost every human problem.

The feeling of being unappreciated at home, of being passed over at work, of being dismissed by our social circles – it is all *nafs*. If we can press the proverbial pause button and remember that we don't work at home to be appreciated, or at work for a promotion, or in social circles to be popular, but rather we work in all three for the pleasure of God – we will finally push beyond our barriers.

Al-Zamalkānī (may God have mercy on him) said, "The barrier of a believer is his *nafs* and his whim. If he opposes them, the barrier will be lifted." We must do our own individual work on our *nafs*. It is not something we can 'borrow' from someone else. It is the hard and real work that finds us getting less sleep, working cheerfully even when we feel slighted, and supporting people of all different backgrounds and behaviors.

We hear much about a spiritual awakening, spiritual highs, and spiritual experiences. Some people will increase their worship, hoping to find those elusive feelings. And while sometimes Allah in His generosity will gift a worshipper rich and real spiritual feelings, the real reaching comes in the fighting of the *nafs*.

A student who attended with Shaikh al-Basṭāmī ﷺ for thirty years said to him, "For thirty years I have attended your sessions while fasting and standing at night, yet even so, I have not tasted any of the inner knowledge of which you speak, though I believe in it and yearn for it." The shaikh said to him, "Were you to fast and pray at night for an eternity, you would not taste of it." He asked, "But why?" He said, "You are barred by your *nafs*."

Practical steps to lessen the power of your *nafs* include:

1. Sleep less and eat less.

2. Be kind to people, putting others before yourself.

3. Be willing to serve without thanks and praise.

4. When there is a bubbling and hard-to-control desire for recognition, or a 'right', or an object, recognize that this is probably your *nafs* and quiet it.

5. Give in charity.

It is important while fighting your *nafs* that you understand it. You should not overburden it only to burn out after a few days. Rather, train your *nafs* to obey you, much the same as an athlete trains her body to perform: a little at a time, but always pushing a little harder. Reward yourself when you have a breakthrough. If you struggle with feeling 'put upon', then the next time you fight that feeling and get over it – offer your *nafs* a little gift (a piece of pie or a new book for example.)

This is a sacred and blessed path. We are fulfilling our purpose in the worship of God and in good deeds. We will not be able to do either, however, if we continue to hold on to that difficult, yet oh-so-comfortable and familiar *nafs*.

May Allah give us all the ability to recognize when our nafs is getting in our way and to deal with it appropriately. May we all taste the sweetness of faith that is pure and clear – free of the murkiness of selfishness and self-righteousness. *Yā Rabb, Āmīn.*

Reflection

Everyone has a couple of areas where their *nafs* proves to be a significant barrier to their spiritual growth. Some people crave recognition, some are lazy, some are selfish, some struggle with jealousy... What roadblock is your *nafs* putting in your path?

Project

Take a look at your *nafs*-related challenges and give something in charity this week with the intention of declaring war on one of them. Ask Allah to help you achieve victory over it and eliminate that barrier. Ask Him to help you remain steadfast in fighting it and to make clear to you the best strategies to do so without being too hard on yourself or too laissez faire. This charity does not have to be monetary, but whatever it is it should involve a real sacrifice. Give a slightly larger amount of money than you are comfortable with, for example, or offer a bit more time to someone than you feel you have, etc.

Reflection / Project

Week 20

Fast Food or
Slow-Roasted Goodness?

E LIVE IN A time where we can take a pill to get rid of our headache, order french-fries to squelch our hunger and use antibacterial wipes to avoid germs. We are surrounded by quick-fixes and immediate satisfactions.

Often, then, we come to Islam and expect to find the same offerings. We look for a 'special' *duʿāʾ* for our heartache, a particular fast for our emptiness, and an answer to our three tears of repentance.

When we do not find what we are looking for within fifteen minutes or a few days of 'trying', we get fed up, begin to fall into despair, and sometimes move on to worldly methods of self-gratification that seem so much easier.

This is not the way of a follower of Muhammad ﷺ.

The companions of the Prophet ﷺ – his first followers – are recorded to have spent many hours in prayer and *duʿāʾ*. They are known to have memorized the Quran early and well. We read of Sālim Mawlā Abī Ḥudhayfa ؓ who, when the Prophet ﷺ heard his recitation said to him, "Praise be to Allah who made from my nation people like you." (*Musnad al-Imām Aḥmad*)

«الحمد لله الذي جعل في أمتي مثلك.»

Sālim was a non-Arab whose early learning of the Quran made him the first to lead the prayer at Qubā'. We read of Abdullah b. 'Umar ﷺ spending long nights in prayer after the Prophet ﷺ mentioned that he was a "good man, if only he would pray at night", and we read of Zainab, Mother of the Believers ﷺ tying a rope in the mosque to hold her up when she tired from a long night of prayer.

Those who followed the companions have similar stories. It is said that Abū Yūsuf, the famous student of Abū Ḥanīfa, would pray two hundred rak'as of extra prayers every day and night. We hear that al-Ḥasan al-Baṣrī wore one cloak for much of his adult life, and when he died it was still in immaculate condition, and that Imām Mālik's student Ibn al-Qāsim would read the entire Quran twice daily for his litany of worship.

These are examples of some of our greatest people, and they did not become our greatest people with a fast-food mentality.

We must rid ourselves of this handicap. We are talking about the most important thing that will ever stand at offer before us: our faith. We must be willing to pour ourselves into its growth and development; we must be willing to withstand a measure of hardship, and we must be willing to do this with a pleasant attitude – an attitude of grateful humility.

Along the way, we must be patient with ourselves. Keep trying, accept failure, work harder. Start each new day with the intention to strive harder, be kinder, fulfill more obligations. We must not look for any spiritual 'feelings' too early in the game. If they occur, they are a gift; if they do not, we recognize that they are a privilege, not a right, and we continue to work. At the same time, do not be deceived by a spiritual moment into thinking, "Aha! I've made it!"

Our growth is woven between the worship that we do, our determination in fighting our *nafs*, and the way we behave towards people. Jābir b. ʿAbdallāh ﷺ reported that the Messenger of God ﷺ said, "Shall I not tell you who the people of paradise are? The people of paradise are everyone who is soft, gentle, easy, and near." (*al-Ṭabarānī*)

عن جابر بن عبد الله قال: قال رسول الله صلى الله عليه وسلم:
«ألا أخبركم بأهل الجنة؟! أهل الجنة كل هين لين سهل قريب.»

We need to smile, be gentle and kind. Avoid arrogance and self-righteous arguing.

We need to pray at the beginning of the time, read Quran, pray at night.

We need to take these threads and painstakingly weave them together into the fabric of our lives. This takes time. It takes effort. It takes determination.

The tapestry of faith is made the old-fashioned way. Let us turn our backs on the fast-food mentality and embrace the joy of slow-roasted goodness.

Reflection

Is there an area of growth where you're frustrated with your lack of progress? Is it that you're waiting for that "spiritual feeling" or a "quick fix"? Is it that you're not patient with yourself?

Project

Choose one act of *ibāda* to add to your daily worship. It can be 100 *ṣalawāt* every day, reading a set number of pages of Quran on a regular basis, adding an extra *sunna*

prayer, an extra set of prayers at *tahajjud*, or any other act of worship. Choose something that is doable and stick with it, for as we know "The most beloved deeds to Allah are those that are consistent, even though they be small."
(*Ṣaḥīḥ Muslim*)

«أحب الأعمال إلى الله تعالى أدومها وإن قل.»

Reflection / Project

Week 21

Fading Faith

I WAS ASKED TO MEET a 'revert' the other day. In this case, I mean an Arab-born Muslim who had traveled to Canada, fallen into sin and denial, then turned toward God through Christianity. She looked at me and said, "A believer knows another believer," and I shuddered. I talked and attempted to understand, but there were closed doors at every turn of the conversation.

A good friend of mine was born a Christian and ran away from overbearing and difficult parents to an Arab husband. She became a Muslim, dragging her husband along with her into religiosity. Then, 25 years later, she dumped it all and returned to her parents – who hadn't changed one bit. I tried to talk to her, too. In that case I was told that I just did not understand.

What is it that steals one's faith?

Faith is a matter of the heart and a matter of the mind. Where it exists there is confidence, and yet with arrogance, it disappears. Trials of this *dunyā* can try one's faith, and too much ease in this *dunyā* can do the same. We are influenced deeply by the people that we meet, spend time with, look up to and open up to. Sometimes it becomes necessary to close the door to those closest to us because their influence will drag us away.

The loss of faith begins with a secret that is harbored in the chest – a secret that opens the door to Shaiṭān, and lends an ear to all that will leave us destroyed. It is the secret that whispers, "I'm not happy – I want to live an easier life." It might say, "My trials were unfairly given to me." It can say, "Why do I have to work so hard when others have it so easy?" Or perhaps, "I'm tired of feeling like an outsider – I just want to be 'normal.'"

The Prophet's ﷺ lifetime was not immune to the trial of loss of faith, though it was less prevalent and more dangerous, since those who entered into Islam had had the privilege of actually knowing the Prophet himself and being part of the connection between the earth and the heavens through revelation. Nonetheless, there are examples of such tragedy.

In the time of the Prophet ﷺ, we find that Umm Ḥabība and her husband went to Abyssinia to escape the abuse and harm of Quraish. There they found relief from persecution. ʿUbaid Allah (Umm Ḥabība's husband) had been a Christian before the beginning of Islam and it seems that either the trial of ease was too much for him, or being surrounded by Christians was more than his faith could bear. One night his wife had a terrible dream, "I saw ʿUbaid Allah – my husband – with a terrible and distorted appearance; I was afraid and said, 'By God, his state has changed.' When ʿUbaid Allah awoke he said to me, 'Oh Umm Ḥabība, I had looked at religions and did not find one better than Christianity, so I converted to it. I then entered the religion of Muhammad, and now I have returned to Christianity.' I said, 'By God, this is not what is good for you,' and I told him of the dream I had seen, but he took no heed, turning to the drinking of wine till his death." (al-Mustadrak)

What was it that pulled him away from the belief in a present prophet? Was it the temptation of this *dunyā*? Was it being of the minority in a country of Christians?

Did he cut himself off from the other Muslim immigrants such that he was not able to carry his faith? It does not seem that he took counsel from his wife, since even her dream had little effect on him. He had met the Prophet ﷺ, endured hardship for the sake of his new religion, and then gave it all up. Even his *dunyā* was destroyed.

We also find the story of Abū Qais b. al-Aslat; he was known in Yathrib (Medina) as one of the Aḥnāf (a handful of people who rejected idolatry and clung to the belief of Ibrāhīm). He was vocal about his beliefs, and spoke of the upcoming prophet. When the Prophet ﷺ came to Medina, Abū Qais's people said to him, "O Abū Qais, here is the person you used to describe to us." He said, "Yes, he has been sent in truthfulness." And he came to the Prophet ﷺ and asked him, "What do you call to?" The Prophet answered, "To the witnessing of no god but God and that I am His Messenger," and he mentioned the laws of Islam.

Abū Qais said, "How good and beautiful this is. I will settle my affairs and return to you." He recognized the truth in Islam, and his previous beliefs were solidified in the person of the Prophet ﷺ. Unfortunately, on his way to 'settle his affairs', he met Abdullah b. Ubayy b. Salūl, who asked him, "Whence from?" He said, "From Muhammad; he presented me with talk so excellent, the same we used to know and the rabbis used to tell us of." Abdullah b. Ubayy said, "By God, you are but loathe to fight the Khazraj." Abū Qais became angry and, wanting to prove he was not adopting Islam to avoid battle out of cowardice, said, "By God, I will not become a Muslim for a whole year!" And he returned to his home. He then died before the year was out. Abū Qais lost out on belief because of the influence of a person. Abdullah b. Ubayy was of the hypocrites of Medina, but Abū Qais heard only personal insult. That slight became more important to him than his belief, and more important to him than following the Prophet ﷺ. (*Ṭabaqāt Ibn Saʿd*)

Abdullah b. Khaṭal was gathering *ṣadaqa* at the Prophet's instruction, when he killed a servant in a fit of temper and then ran away from Islam, and assumedly, his conscience. He could not face the Prophet ﷺ, could not face Allah, could not face the reality of his sin, so he chose escape instead. His sin was great – indeed murder is of the worst of sins – but his turning away from Islam was worse still. Had he faced the Prophet ﷺ, he would have met with his just rewards, which would most likely have been a grave punishment here in the *dunyā*, but in the *ākhira* may have been forgiveness and acceptance.

Three differing incidents where faith was lost – three clear causes: weakness or lack of steadfastness, the opinion of others or a challenge to one's pride, and sin that dragged the otherwise sound of mind to great and terrible loss.

When faced with a person who has lost her faith, take stock. Recognize and know that of all the trials available to humanity, she has suffered the most – indeed her suffering is not over. Do not react in arrogance, but in humility. Ask yourself what you could have done to help her, ask yourself what you are doing to protect yourself.

Reflection

Do you know anyone who has lost his or her faith? If so, how did you react? Is there anything you feel you could have done, or could still do, to try and influence him/her to remain within the folds of Islam and begin a path of spiritual growth?

Project

Examine your heart for secret thoughts that might weaken your faith and seek refuge with Allah from them. If you have any serious questions about Islam, write to me this week and ask me your questions (anse@rabata.org) or consider registering in the class Foundations, Flounderings and Faith. This class was designed to address questions and challenges of faith for the modern Muslim woman (Rabata.org/ribaat).

Reflection / Project

....

$\mathcal{W}eek$ 22

....

Keeping Faith

*O*UR MEDIA CULTURE HAS raised us to believe things about faith, things that are not part of the Islamic outlook. We have been raised to believe that people of faith should be 'perfect' – they should not make glaring errors. Thus, if a new Muslim, or newly practicing Muslim, witnesses that of which she disapproves, doubt insidiously enters her heart. We have been raised to believe that pleasure is quick and immediate, so working hard to achieve religiosity seems incongruent with what we 'know'. We have been raised to believe that we are terribly important – that somehow our opinions matter greatly in the scheme of the world. Modern culture would have each of us developing our own religion and religiosity – our own individual way of seeking 'peace', each and every one of us a 'pharaoh' in our own way.

We have also been raised to believe in the disposability of all things. Along with paper plates and newspapers, people can be disposed of – lives can be recycled – and nothing is really important enough to sacrifice for.

Faith, however, is not disposable. It must not be lost because of the influence of any other human being, no matter how close to us they may be – not those who call us to another faith, nor those who laugh at the faith we have. We must not seek after an image – but rather a reality. The image of the 'happy go-lucky' non-Muslim is one created by the media and our imagination. The truth is that our happiness and peace are directly related to our faith and the deeds that support that faith.

We must cling to our faith with both hands, as the Prophet ﷺ says, 'hold on with our teeth.' We must turn our faces away from those that tempt us to another lifestyle. We must run with our hands over our ears from that which whispers to us to give up, or that which asks us to give victory to our *nafs* instead of our faith. Faith is our most valuable asset, more valuable than our children, our jobs, our spouses, our homes, our money, our jewelry, our friends, our positions... It is more valuable than all of the things that we give our days and nights to. Faith is not disposable. Cling to it with every cell of your body, your heart and your soul.

Islam has given us the tools we need to clutch our faith to our chests. In adhering to that which is *farḍ*, and abstaining from *ḥarām*, we protect ourselves and avoid the sins that might otherwise take us down a dangerous path. In filling our minds with the Quran and its meanings, with knowledge of the life of the Prophet ﷺ, and with basic knowledge of the Islamic sciences, we build a fortress against that which seeks to create doubt. In keeping to the Islamic schedule of prayer and worship, we create a heart that burns brightly and cannot be put out by the winds of opinion and personal sensitivities.

Look to your life and the lives of those around you. Create homes that pulsate with halal and repel *ḥarām*. Fill days with learning and teaching, fill nights with worship and tears. Call upon your Lord to protect you and your loved ones from the worst and most difficult trial of all – the trial of a challenge to your faith.

Reflection

We all say that faith is the most important thing in our lives, but sometimes we manifest a different reality – when push comes to shove, we actually prioritize other things above our religion. Is this happening to you? Is there anything you are valuing more than your faith? For example, are people's opinions stopping you from wearing hijab? Is the priority of a solid eight hours of sleep preventing you from waking every morning for Fajr? Is your desire to be right inhibiting you from repairing a damaged relationship? Take stock of yourself and identify the areas where you need to re-center your focus on your faith.

Project

Make a list of ten faith myths and/or relationship myths that you may have bought into (or carried with you out of your pre-Islam days). Maybe somewhere in your heart you believe the "happily ever after" myth or cling to the superiority of studying random verses of scripture every week instead of building a strong, overall foundation with the Qur'an. For each myth, write how you can go about countering it. Reach out for help with that if you need to.

Reflection / Project

Week 23

Spring in Every Season

*I*N KINDERGARTEN, TEACHERS TEACH the seasons. They tell children that summer is hot and sunny, and that it is a time of play and fun. Autumn is a time of changing leaves and apples and pumpkins. Winter is snowy white, cold and spent mostly indoors. Spring is flowers and renewal, misty rain and lots of smiles.

Children learn that times change, nothing very good or very bad stays forever. The leaves will fall and the snow will melt. In upper-elementary school, seasons of the year are replaced with seasons of life, as literature and social studies come into a child's life and they read about dastardly deeds and heroic hearts.

Muslims experience the seasons as a continuous gift from God:

Verily in the creation of the heavens and the earth, and the alternation of night and day – there are indeed signs for people of understanding... (3:190)

إِنَّ فِي خَلْقِ ٱلسَّمَٰوَٰتِ وَٱلْأَرْضِ وَٱخْتِلَٰفِ ٱلَّيْلِ وَٱلنَّهَارِ لَآيَٰتٍ لِّأُوْلِي ٱلْأَلْبَٰبِ ۝

115

The tall trees of late fall that stand like soldiers but move like lace are a sign of the coming cold. In late March, winter threatens to stay. Flowers trying to peek out from the cold earth are losing the battle. Trees try to blossom, but snowflakes cover the pink buds. It is a time 'in-between' – not quite winter, and not quite spring. Then the snow finally melts and the summer sun bakes the earth, granting long days romping at the seaside and long evenings talking under the darkening sky.

Verily with hardship there is ease. (94:6)

$$ \text{إِنَّ مَعَ ٱلْعُسْرِ يُسْرًا ﴿٦﴾} $$

Our human seasons come and go in similar ways: graduation, marriage, birth, a new job, a big move... Sometimes life stages and events come and go with the same joy as the seasons, and at other times we stagnate. Our night prayers, like the flowers, threaten to give up the fight. Our positive attitude, carefully honed, is blanketed with the burdens of life's trials. It is here that *sabr* becomes our rope.

Sabr is commonly translated as 'patience'. But the word patience in Western life is used to teach us how to wait. We are taught to wait our turn, wait in line, wait for a call, wait and wait. While this might be patience, it is not *sabr*. *Sabr* is determination; it is not giving up; it is little flowers opening up in defiance of snowflakes. *Sabr* is the fragile smile that holds on, even though illness, distance, and poverty threaten on the horizon.

Khadīja ﷺ was the personification of *sabr*. She demonstrated great *sabr* during the fifteen years she waited for her husband to receive the *waḥī*. Those years were filled with long days alone, the death of two infant sons, and the day-to-day hardships of life. Then when the revelation finally began, she chose the *daʿwa*. She continued to live in forbearance when the *mushrikīn* of Mecca began to find ways to hurt the Prophet 🕌 and, by default, Khadīja. Two of her daughters found themselves rejected and divorced, garbage was thrown outside her doorstep daily, and her husband had the innards of a slaughtered animal thrown on him in prayer. She kept working in support of the *da'wa* and the Prophet 🕌 as she watched and heard of the abuse and torture that was inflicted upon her people. When the Muslims were corralled into the cols of Mecca, starved and ostracized – she joined them in facing starvation and danger. Her money paid purposely inflated prices for food and her disposition gave hope to the other Muslims. Khadīja 🕌 died in that season. While the other Muslims were to see the spring of the *da'wa*, with a move to Medina, victory at Badr, and a growing *umma*, Khadīja's physical life ended in the dark season of the boycott. Yet her very personage has given Muslim men and women a reason to hope every day since her death.

In our personal lives, we can sometimes feel as though spring will never come, that it will still be snowing in July. It can seem as though we will never see our loved ones again, or that we will never be able meet our debts. It can seem that illness is forever, or painful relationships are our destiny. It is at this time that we must draw from the wellspring of *ṣabr* – we must pull out hope and trust. We must keep going – keep doing the same thing day after day. Like Khadīja 🕌, we may have to pay inflated prices, we may have to serve our religion while others try to destroy it, and we may have to be ready to embrace the hurt and frightened around us. For in truth, our seasons extend into the next life, where Khadīja 🕌 found her spring, and that alone gives us hope. Let us remember the lessons of kindergarten and elementary school: seasons come and go, and nothing of this world lasts forever. As we wait for our own personal spring, we must grab onto the rope of *sabr*, knowing that if we hold on tight enough, the rope itself will take us where we need to be.

Reflection

"I am amazed by the believer. If he is granted goodness, he praises Allah and is grateful. If he is afflicted with a calamity, he praises Allah and is patient. The believer is rewarded for every matter, even lifting a morsel of food to his wife's mouth." (Musnad al-Imām Aḥmad)

«عجبت للمؤمن، إذا أصابه خير حمد الله وشكر، وإن أصابته مصيبة حمد الله وصبر، فالمؤمن يؤجر في كل أمره حتى يؤجر في اللقمة يرفعها الى في امرأته.»

What season are you in at the moment? Are you in a joyous celebration of spring, a crisp, busy autumn or a dreary, seemingly endless winter? Are you using *sabr* to find the hope of spring, like Khadīja ﷺ?

Project

If you are going through a winter, or if you can remember one, sit down and think about the situation - about all its facets and variables, its genesis, and its possible resolutions. Now, imagine that someone else has just described that situation to you. Write down what advice you would give.

Reflection / Project

Week 24

Soap for the Mouth

T HE BIRDS ARE SINGING in the morning and freshness perfumes the air and stirs your spirit. Spring has sprung. Many women will begin to eye their stuffy homes with mop and scrub brush in hand. Warm and toasty woolen blankets will begin to look unbearable, and will be washed and packed away. Spring cleaning lightens everyone's mood and revitalizes our environments.

Housecleaning and spiritual cleaning have always been both allegorical and closely intertwined for me. So spring cleaning tends to draw me inward, looking for the musty and dusty, the heavy and the unbearable.

One of the signs of a believer is that she does not partake in idle talk, and certainly not sinful talk. A believer has a wholesome tongue. Allah the Most High reminds us:

He does not utter a single word without a watcher by him, pen in hand. (50:18)

مَّا يَلْفِظُ مِن قَوْلٍ إِلَّا لَدَيْهِ رَقِيبٌ عَتِيدٌ ۝

And the Prophet ﷺ has warned us that, "Anyone who believes in Allah and the Last Day should speak good or be silent." (*Ṣaḥīḥ al-Bukhārī and Muslim*)

«ومن كان يؤمن بالله واليوم الآخر فليقل خيراً أو ليصمت.»

Let us spring clean our tongues with *dhikr* Allah. Let us wash away our hurtful words with the beautiful words of the Quran. Sacred months are upon us; let us be free of the darkness and filth of out-of-control talking. There is no excuse for an unbridled tongue (or fingers on the keyboard) – not exhaustion, not poor circumstances, not even anger.

In the season of spring cleaning, then, let us look at the types of tongues we should be scrubbing and buffing.

Tongues in need of soap:

The Lying tongue

Abū Huraira ﷺ tells us that the Prophet ﷺ said, "Three things are signs of the hypocrite: when he speaks he tells lies, when he promises he breaks it and when he is trusted he proves to be dishonest." (*Saḥīḥ al-Bukhārī and Muslim*)

«آية المنافق ثلاث: إذا حدث كذب،
وإذا وعد أخلف، وإذا اؤتمن خان.»

The worst kind of person to be is a hypocrite. If you hear yourself telling a lie, whether as a joke or a flat out untruth, stop. Stand back. Be silent. If the truth is difficult, it is better to say nothing than to engage in lying.

The Argumentative Tongue

Abū Umāma al-Bāhilī tells us that the Prophet ﷺ said, "I guarantee a house in Janna for one who gives up arguing, even if he is in the right; and I guarantee a home in the middle of Janna for one who abandons lying even for the sake of fun; and I guarantee a house in the highest part of Janna for one who improves his manners." (*Sunan Abī Dawūd*)

»أنا زعيمٌ ببيتٍ في ربض الجنة لمن ترك المراء وإن كان محقّاً، وببيتٍ في وسط الجنة، لمن ترك الكذب وإن كان مازحاً، وببيتٍ في أعلى الجنة لمن حسَّن خلقه.«

Arguing removes the blessing from relationships. A tongue that is quick to anger and quick to argue is not a tongue on its way to paradise. Instead of argument: action. If you are in the right, good action will prove it better than a thousand words. Instead of argument: humbleness. If you are in the right, there is no need for the world to know. Truth makes itself known eventually. Instead of argument: quietude. Silent reflection often brings about a deeper truth, so that even if you were right to a degree, the quietness can further that. We lost the blessing of Lailat al-Qadr because of foolish argument[1]. Let us hold on to our blessings with peaceful avoidance of arguing.

---

1   'Ubāda b. al-Ṣāmit narrates in *Ṣaḥīḥ al-Bukhārī*, "The Prophet ﷺ came out to inform us of Lailat al-Qadr, but two men of the Muslims argued, so he ﷺ said, 'I came out to inform you of Lailat al-Qadr, but so-and-so and so-and-so argued, so it was lifted, and perhaps that is better for you. Search for it on the [twenty] ninth and the [twenty] seventh and the [twenty] fifth.'"

خرج النبي صلى الله عليه وسلم ليخبرنا بليلة القدر، فتلاحى رجلان من المسلمين، فقال: »خرجت لأخبركم بليلة القدر، فتلاحى فلان وفلان فرفعت، وعسى أن يكون خيرا لكم، فالتمسوها في التاسعة والسابعة والخامسة.«

The Complaining Tongue

The Prophet ﷺ said, "Who believes in God and the Last Day, let him speak good or be silent."
(*Ṣaḥīḥ al-Bukhārī and Muslim*)

«ومن كان يؤمن بالله واليوم الآخر فليقل خيرًا أو ليصمت.»

We must not let our tongues begin the day with complaints and end the day with more complaints. How many good things do we say in one day? How many negative? May Allah forgive us. Let us train our tongues to say that which is beautiful, or to be silent.

There are more tongues in need of a good scrub: the manipulating tongue, the hasty tongue, the divisive tongue, the boasting tongue, the slandering tongue, the gossiping tongue, the meddling tongue, the betraying tongue, the belittling tongue, the cynical tongue, the know-it-all tongue, the harsh tongue, the rude tongue, the judgmental tongue, the cursing and swearing tongue, the accusing tongue, the discouraging tongue, the doubting tongue, the indiscreet tongue, and the yelling and shouting tongue.

To name a few.

For good measure, let us remember that our fingers affect our heart just as our tongue does, when they are the instruments of our speech. Do not work hard to control your tongue and then allow your fingers to fall into ugly and un-Islamic discussions and statements online.

Five steps to spring cleaning our speech:

1. *Tawba* (repentance) from previous comments.

2. Seeking forgiveness from people (not for backbiting – in this case you make things right by speaking kindly about the person to the same audience).

3. Pushing the pause button. Before you speak, count to ten, send peace and blessings on the Prophet 	, or make *wuḍū'*, breathe, then speak with *taqwā*.

4. Practice silence in a quiet atmosphere and in a talkative atmosphere. Listen carefully to people, and speak less often rather than more often.

5. Fill your mouth and fingers with words and phrases of the remembrance of Allah, either in reminding yourself or in reaching out to others.

May this spring be the season of budding beauty within our hearts and souls. Prepare the way for this beauty with a good, soapy scrub of the tongue.

Reflection

Is your tongue inclined to any of the types of speech listed above? Think back to your conversations during the past 24 hours. Did your speech reflect any of those qualities? If so, what do you think was your motivation? Love of position? Wishing to be liked by people? Low self esteem? Were you trying to ingratiate yourself with one person or group by making disparaging remarks against another? Analyze why you might feel the temptation to speak unkindly about others.

Project

There's a common misconception that if you have spoken ill of someone you remedy that by admitting it to them. This is not how we build healthy relationships or communities. Instead, the way to repair any damage you have done by speaking ill of someone is to speak well of them in the same company. Think of someone you may have spoken ill of and dedicate this week to making up for it. Speak good about them to the same audience. This does not have to be disingenuous – we all have good qualities and bad qualities, good deeds and not-so-good ones. Find that person's good qualities and/or good deeds and talk them up!

Reflection / Project

_____

_____

_____

_____

_____

_____

_____

_____

_____

_____

_____

_____

_____

_____

_____

_____

_____

_____

_____

_____

_____

Week 25

Taxes

LL GOVERNMENTS REQUIRE PEOPLE to pay taxes of some type. In the USA the yearly filing of income tax reports involves lots of form filling and hair pulling.

What if we were to look at the blessings of Allah upon us as income? And then extrapolated upon that to think about what 'tax' we owe upon them? What if we had a yearly deadline in which to 'report' on our previous year's 'blessings income' and 'tax payout'? What would that form look like?

There would be the general form. The one where we report on the blessings of our humanity:

And We have certainly honored the children of Adam and carried them on the land and sea and provided for them of the good things and preferred them over much of what We have created, with [definite] preference. (17:70)

﷽ وَلَقَدْ كَرَّمْنَا بَنِي ءَادَمَ وَحَمَلْنَٰهُمْ فِى ٱلْبَرِّ وَٱلْبَحْرِ وَرَزَقْنَٰهُم مِّنَ ٱلطَّيِّبَٰتِ وَفَضَّلْنَٰهُمْ عَلَىٰ كَثِيرٍ مِّمَّنْ خَلَقْنَا تَفْضِيلًا ﴿٧٠﴾

We would mention the blessing of our ability to think and reason:

And Allah has extracted you from the wombs of your mothers not knowing a thing, and He made for you hearing and vision and intellect that perhaps you would be grateful, (16:78)

وَٱللَّهُ أَخْرَجَكُم مِّنۢ بُطُونِ أُمَّهَٰتِكُمْ لَا تَعْلَمُونَ شَيْـًٔا وَجَعَلَ لَكُمُ ٱلسَّمْعَ وَٱلْأَبْصَٰرَ وَٱلْأَفْـِٔدَةَ لَعَلَّكُمْ تَشْكُرُونَ

The blessings of the environment and beauty around us:

O humankind, worship your Lord, who created you and those before you, that you may become righteous – [He] who made for you the earth a bed [spread out] and the sky a ceiling an d sent down from the sky rain, and brought forth thereby fruits as provision for you... (2:21-22)

يَٰٓأَيُّهَا ٱلنَّاسُ ٱعْبُدُواْ رَبَّكُمُ ٱلَّذِى خَلَقَكُمْ وَٱلَّذِينَ مِن قَبْلِكُمْ لَعَلَّكُمْ تَتَّقُونَ ۝ ٱلَّذِى جَعَلَ لَكُمُ ٱلْأَرْضَ فِرَٰشًا وَٱلسَّمَآءَ بِنَآءً وَأَنزَلَ مِنَ ٱلسَّمَآءِ مَآءً فَأَخْرَجَ بِهِۦ مِنَ ٱلثَّمَرَٰتِ رِزْقًا لَّكُمْ

Then the form especially for Muslims would need filling out: The blessing of faith and Islam:

They consider it a favor to you that they have accepted Islam. Say, "Do not consider your Islam a favor to me. Rather, Allah has conferred favor upon you that He has guided you to the faith, if you should be truthful." (49:17)

يَمُنُّونَ عَلَيْكَ أَنْ أَسْلَمُوا۟ قُل لَّا تَمُنُّوا۟ عَلَىَّ إِسْلَـٰمَكُم ۖ بَلِ ٱللَّهُ يَمُنُّ عَلَيْكُمْ أَنْ هَدَىٰكُمْ لِلْإِيمَـٰنِ إِن كُنتُمْ صَـٰدِقِينَ ﴿١٧﴾

The blessing of our sisterhood, and the support of one another, the blessing of recognizing each other at the store, and the stretched heart of love:

...and remember the favor of Allah upon you – when you were enemies and He brought your hearts together, and you became, by His favor, brothers... (3:103)

وَٱذْكُرُوا۟ نِعْمَتَ ٱللَّهِ عَلَيْكُمْ إِذْ كُنتُمْ أَعْدَآءً فَأَلَّفَ بَيْنَ قُلُوبِكُمْ فَأَصْبَحْتُم بِنِعْمَتِهِۦٓ إِخْوَٰنًا

All of the blessings of certainty, spiritual peace, serendipitous events, purity of body and heart, longing and love for the Prophet ﷺ, remembrance of God – indeed every single internal blessing would have a spot on that form.

Finally our personal form, the one where we fill out our secret blessings, would need to be completed. Squares to check our full refrigerator, our new computer, our beautiful desk, the diet that works, the husband that listens, the child that prays, and the coffee pot that fills the house with the rich smell of 'awake'. On and on and on...

Once the forms are filled out, it is time to calculate what we owe. Have we prayed enough? Given enough *ṣadaqa*? Called others to Islam? Smiled and been kind? Brought joy to others? Have we done anything 'enough'?

How much do we owe?

Form in hand, one day, we will indeed be faced with our audit. May Allah ﷻ make us of those whose blessings are apparent in our state of mind, state of heart and our daily deeds. *Āmīn.*

Reflection

What are the kinds of blessings that you have personally been granted? If you were to be audited and the ones you owe taxes on were to be repossessed, how many would you have left? Think of one or two ways you could go about paying taxes on your blessings.

Project

Choose a secret deed to do this week as a down payment on your 'taxes' owed. Some people have done things like cleaning up their mosque and brightening it with flowers, visiting an elderly person, knitting a blanket for refugee children, or sending an anonymous care package.

Once you have done your deed, try to devise a way you can take it forward with you into the future and make it a regular habit. Maybe you could knit a blanket a month, bring flowers to the mosque every Friday or sponsor an orphan for a year via automatic withdrawal.

Your secret deed will ease your audit on the Day of Judgment!

Reflection / Project

Week 26

A Simple Formula

ANYTIME YOU WONDER HOW big your round dining room table is, all you have to do is take the radius, square it and multiply it by Pi. If you want to know the size of your pizza, same formula: πr^2.

Not only circles, but other complicated math problems can be solved with simple formulas. The same formula plugged into a problem about the chance of finding a good husband in a small town in Georgia can be used to find the probability of finding your favorite brand of popcorn at the corner store. Math is amazing.

Once, when I was young, I had a long conversation with a friend of mine about the difference between the math of the world and the math of the spiritual existence. I waxed on and on about how things just don't always make sense. "one plus one does not always equal two," I said, and my friend and I nodded together at my wisdom.

Later that day I was attending a *sira* class, and I said to the instructor when she inquired about my day, "Today I realized something so important." What was it? She wanted to know. "I realized that in our spiritual growth, one plus one doesn't always equal two. And that thinking it does is the root of our frustration."

She looked at me with eyes that showed both amusement and pity. "That's ridiculous," she said, "one plus one always equals two. The issue at hand is that you must have both of the ones." And with that, my ethereal thinking was tossed out the window.

And, of course, she was right.

Just as math is reliable, our spiritual growth is dependent on certain formulas for success. We will not grow if we do not wake up for *tahajjud*. We will wither and lose ground if we are missing *fard* prayers. We will backslide if we do not make a conscious effort to work and strive in the path of God and His prophet ﷺ. We will shrivel if we allow this *dunyā* to overtake our time, our concern, our emotions. One plus one equals two.

Of course, while mathematical formulas are reliable, we cannot use the formula for the area of a circle in order to find the area of a triangle. Likewise, if we have a problem with our *nafs* – if we are selfish or stingy, for example – we will not solve it with fasting. If we are lacking *tawfīq* (serendipitous fortune) because we are missing *fard* prayers, we will not suddenly happen upon it by giving in charity.

Our religion is clear and beautiful, like the clarity of a mathematical formula. It is up to us to identify which formula we need to use, and to make sure that before we whine and complain about the results of our problem (it is not two!), that we have been sure to add one plus one.

Reflection

Is there a place where you know you are not giving your full self? Where your "ones" are not really both present? Sometimes we try to achieve spiritual health while feeding our bodies food bought with money that is tainted with usury or other haram dealings. Sometimes we yearn for success in our academic studies while neglecting to spend any time with the Quran. Examine one of your goals and try to find variables that may be preventing you from reaching it – places where your ones are perhaps more like halves or zeroes. Think wide and deep: the connections may not be immediately obvious.

Project

Brush up on your spiritual math.

Getting up for Fajr = staying away from *ḥarām* during the day + going to bed on time + sleeping with *wuḍū* + making *duʿā* about it.

Write a similar equation for a spiritual goal you're trying to reach. Think about things you might be missing – do you have all the components to make a true equation? Identify what's missing and work on factoring it in this week.

Reflection / Project

Week 27

Rajab and *Tawba*

IN 1985 I WAS a brand new Muslim and Ramadan came in the summer. It was hot. It was humid. I was fasting. It was the most wonderful month of my life. As years passed, Ramadan moved into the winter, but every year when the temperature began to creep up I would sniff the air and feel that Ramadan was near.

The Islamic calendar brings with it that which helps us 'sniff the air'. Every year the two months that precede Ramadan arrive to greet us and escort us into that most loving of months: Ramadan.

Rajab, a month of *tawba* (repentance) and Sha'bān, a month of reconciliation.

Anas b. Mālik ♛ said that the Prophet ♛ would say at the beginning of Rajab, "O God, bless us in Rajab and Sha'bān and bless us in Ramadan." (*Musnad al-Imām Aḥmad*)

«كان النبي صلى الله عليه وسلم إذا دخل رجب قال: اللهم بارك لنا في رجب وشعبان وبارك لنا في رمضان.»

Rajab is a sacred month. The practice of the sanctification of months goes back to Prophet Ibrāhīm ♛ and was affirmed by Prophet Muhammad ♛. These are months in which killing is forbidden and safety and peace reign.

Rajab is also the month in which Prophet Muhammad ﷺ was given the gift of the Isrāʾ and Miʿrāj – his trip to Jerusalem and to the heavens.

Rajab, according to many of the ʿulamāʾ, is a month of repentance and forgiveness. If we are to consider that Ramadan is right around the corner, and that a requirement of our faith is tawba (repentance), then it makes excellent sense to utilize Rajab, a month of peace, to make peace with our Lord, to seek forgiveness, and to offer a complete tawba.

Tawba:

> Allah ﷻ says: *O you who believe, repent to Allah, a genuine repentance.* (66:8)

We who claim to believe are required to continuously repent from our sins, our mistakes, our shortcomings: all that stands in the way of a life of joy and light under the shade of God's pleasure. Too often, we are so involved in seeing the wrongful deeds of others that we have a limited view of our own shortcomings. Rajab offers us the opportunity to forget about everyone else's sins for a while and focus on our own. It is worthwhile to spend some time before Rajab in retreat and reflection... Where are you with Allah? Where is Islam in your life? Compare your state this month with your state last year before Ramadan: are you closer to Allah or further away?

✓ Questions to ask:

1. Am I attached to a particular sin?

Do I read, watch, or listen to ḥarām? Do I read chick lit or sexually explicit books? Do I listen to music that turns my heart toward haram feelings and actions?

Do I watch internet videos that need to be turned off when someone enters my room?

2. Is there a basic of Islam that I take lightly (don't find very important)?

Do I sleep through Fajr prayer every day? Do I wear clothing that the Prophet ﷺ would disapprove of? Do I neglect zakat by saying to myself, "I pay a lot in charity – I don't have to worry about zakat."? Yet zakat is the *fard* (required act), and charity is the *sunna* (extra deed).

3. Do I neglect my basic duties?

If I am a student, do I neglect my studying, leaving it to the last minute and then "cramming"? If I am an employee, am I often late to work? Or do I barely do my job, taking as many breaks as possible? Regarding any relationships (marital, parental, familial or friendship) do I give my all? Or do I hold back, checking to see what I am getting in return?

4. Do I have my priorities straight?

How do I spend my time? Do I waste more time than I use productively? Do I measure ideas and lifestyles against Islam instead of the other way around? Do I spend more time on Facebook than on religious duties?

5. Is there something in my very character that I need to work on?

Am I stubborn? Am I stingy? Stingy with money? Stingy with emotion? Stingy with time? Am I cynical? Do I have a negative outlook on life and therefore on the blessings of Allah?

The truth is that *tawba* is never-ending because we, as human beings, make mistakes; we fall short; we sin. It is true that along the way our sins and mistakes will (should) change as we learn to avoid some, and then find ourselves falling into others. We will then have to make *tawba* from the new sins…and the process goes on. There will never come a day when any one of us reaches perfection.

Thus, Rajab is a gift to us – a time to reflect on the past year, to seek forgiveness from Allah ﷻ, to wash away the darkness of distance and wrongdoing. It is a month to prepare for the upcoming opportunity of Ramadan.

Our *tawba* in the month of Rajab is a breeze that, if collected together, could be the gale that is needed to lift our *umma*, for the forgiveness of each of us adds to the release of our *umma* from hardship. May Allah ﷻ accept our repentance, forgive us, and bless us, our families, and our countries with His miracle.

The Prophet ﷺ said, "Repent to Allah; indeed I repent one hundred times per day." (*al-Suyūṭī*)

«استغفروا ربكم، إني أستغفر الله وأتوب إليه كل يوم مائة مرة.»

Thus, the repetition of '*astaghfirullāh*' was a habit of our Prophet ﷺ – he who was forgiven and promised the reward of his Lord. Over time, the *ʿulamā*ʾ have, through experience, set the number 70,000 as a goal to be reached in the month of Rajab. In order to reach 70,000 *istighfār* in the month of Rajab, you will need to do approximately 2,500 per day. These can be divided into the prayers (500 each prayer) or the morning and evening (1250 morning, and 1250 evening) or just done throughout the day. Together we can make our individual and our collective *tawba*. May Allah accept it! *Āmīn*.

Reflection

Run through the questions in the essay. Is there one that particularly rings true for you? Is there a particular area in which you feel you need to make *tawba* or, on the other hand, are there things you know you are doing wrong but for which you do not really feel the need to seek forgiveness? Part of the definition of a healthy heart is one that feels remorse acutely and strives always to cleanse any black spots before they have time to "set in". Is this an area you need to work on?

Project

Focus this coming month on making 2,500 *istighfār* each day, and on cleansing your heart of sins you may have fallen into since last Ramadan. Do you feel lighter? Cleaner? You may not at first. And that's OK. Spiritual growth is not necessarily something that affects you emotionally right away. But just as a runner must condition her body through daily workouts in order to stay competitive, a seeker must condition her heart through daily *dhikr* and other worship in order to cure her heart. And just as a runner sometimes hits plateaus that she has to push through if she ever wants to run that marathon, so the seeker may also find herself stuck at one stage or another – and pushing through to the next level usually involves a lot of work before the rewards are felt.

Reflection / Project

_____

_____

_____

_____

_____

_____

_____

_____

_____

_____

_____

_____

_____

_____

_____

_____

_____

_____

_____

_____

_____

_____

Week 28

Rajab Shopping

OMETIMES IT FEELS OVERWHELMING to think about becoming a better person. "I'm ok," resonates easily in the breast and our 'busyness' helps us avoid thinking about it. But we have happened upon the month of Rajab, and with it a golden opportunity.

While every month should be a month of peace, righteousness and piety, the four sacred months have been favored over the other months, and they provide us with an opportunity to make real changes in our behavior. Ibn ʿAbbās ؓ said, "Allah distinguished these four months, made them sacred, and glorified them; He made sinning during them of worse consequence than during the others, and the reward for righteous deeds is greater."

There are four sacred months: Dhū al-Qiʿda, Dhū al-Ḥijja, Muḥarram and Rajab. Dhū al-Qiʿda is a month of preparing for the pilgrimage, Dhū al-Ḥijja includes the pilgrimage, and Muḥarram is returning from the pilgrimage. Rajab stands alone.

Rajab is like a big "Black Friday" sale, but it lasts for an entire month instead of just one day. So make your list and get shopping.

Start your Rajab shopping with your mornings. Have you joined the *tahajjud* revolution yet? Has it been a year (at least) since you last missed Fajr? Start Rajab by becoming a person of *tahajjud*, and *in shā' Allah* next year you will look back upon a year of 'on time' Fajrs.

Add a clean and tranquil home to your shopping cart. Is it neat and tidy? Does it smell good? Are the voices peaceful and the words pleasant? Do not delay your spring cleaning until Ramadan and pre-Eid – begin now. As you clean up and clear up, plan ways to turn your house into an angel magnet.

Be gentle with the people in your home. They are a sacred trust to you; their feelings and their hearts lie quivering in your hands. Set aside your *nafs* and turn with an open heart to their service and love.

Double check your cart and make sure you are leaving behind the habits of sin you have fallen into. Tight clothes (men and women) and immodesty, stinginess and bitterness, lies and slander, crabbiness and arrogance all need to be left behind. Their cost is too high.

When you stand at the 'checkout' line on the last day of Rajab, be sure to have gathered plenty of fasting days, lots of *istighfār*, and copious amounts of *du'ā'*. This is the currency you will use to leave the month cleansed of sin, energized with righteousness, and truly blessed by this month of blessings.

Reflection

Read through the Rajab shopping list in the essay. How many of these do you have in your cart? Reflect on each of them and decide what you can add, what you need more of or, conversely, what you need to put back.

Project

Having a peaceful home is like having a recharge pad. It allows you to recharge so you have energy to expend in other areas of your life like work, service, social responsibilities and worship. The best way to create a peaceful home is to make your home an "angel magnet". Angels are attracted to *dhikr* (remembrance of Allah), *sitr* (modesty), *'itr* (nice scents) and *ṭuhr* (clean, purified spaces). Concentrate this week on shaping up your home to be attractive to angels – their presence will help you afford the shiny new habits on your Rajab shopping list.

Reflection / Project

Week 29

Celebrate Our Many Mothers

W HEN THE PROPHET ﷺ buried Fāṭima bint Asad, he prayed for her and called her "my mother".

There were many reasons for this, not the least of which is that she had raised him when, after his grandfather Abd al-Muṭṭalib died, he had gone to live with his uncle Abū Ṭālib.

She was also one of the first to believe. In an intellectually independent move, she diverged from her husband's stance of, "I cannot leave what my forefathers believed in," and followed Prophet Muhammad ﷺ in faith.

She turned her belief toward her children, and all of them entered Islam. We know and love all of her children and two of them are especially dear to our hearts: Jaʿfar b. Abī Ṭālib and ʿAlī b. Abī Ṭālib (may Allah be pleased with both of them).

She followed the Prophet ﷺ to Medina and her home was a place of rest for him there. She also became the mother-in-law of the Prophet's daughter when her son ʿAlī ﷺ married his daughter Fāṭima ﷺ.

This woman was called 'my mother' by our dear Prophet ﷺ as a term of honor, respect and gratitude for the fact that she mothered him, even though they weren't biologically related, for mothering, like love, is a verb.

146

Who is your mother? Who are the women in your life who have cared for you in your childhood? Who are the women who have set strong examples of intellectual clarity and belief? Who are the women who were devoted to *da'wa* and the guidance of those around them? Who are your mothers?

The woman who gave birth to you is especially deserving of your kindness, prayer and loyalty. Do not be impatient with her quirks and demands, rather celebrate them and fulfill them.

The aunts and grandmothers who crave to know about your lives and wish you had more time for them, but forgive you for being 'busy', are also deserving of your attention and time.

The teachers who worried about your prayers and your learning, wherever they are, have a right to your appreciation and fulfillment of the trust.

Friends and sisters who have listened to you and loved you even when you struggled to spend time with them deserve your gratitude and prayers.

Neighbor women, community women and boss women – all the women who contributed to mothering you – they deserve your loyal thanks.

Let us pause and remember all the wonderful women in our lives. Hold the memory and be thankful. *Allāhu Akbar* and *al-ḥamdu l-i-Llāh* for all the women who have loved and cared for us – even if the way they showed it was neither blithe nor decorous. Take five minutes a day and call them on the telephone, send a card, make some effort to show them that you are not ungrateful. Indeed the Prophet ﷺ said, "He does not thank God, who does not thank people." (*Sunan al-Tirmidhī*)

«من لا يَشكُرِ النَّاسَ لا يَشكُرِ اللهَ.»

With a full and thankful heart, let us then pray for our mothers this week. All the women who have helped us become the women we are today; let us not be of those who forget and are disloyal. Let us pray for them. In the still of the night, let us raise our hands and pray for them deeply and fervently.

Yā Rabb, Āmīn.

Reflection

Think of all the women who have helped you grow along the way. List the ways they have been there for you.

Think of your own mother. How did the way she raised you make you into the person you are today? Was her guidance direct or was it her mistakes that you learned the most from? Even if your childhood was not idyllic, perhaps now as an adult you can empathize more or understand your mother's actions better. Are you at a place yet where you can be grateful for her mistakes as well as the things she did well?

Project

Sit down this week and write or call the women in your life who have mothered you along the way. Try to remember a particular act or habit of theirs that affected you and thank them for it explicitly – imagine how they will feel when they hear that their (probably forgotten) actions had such an impact on you! Then get out your planner and pencil in fifteen minutes each week to reach out to one of them.

Reflection / Project

Week 30

Messy Closets and Rajab

AJAB CAN BE A tough month for many people. It begins, this month of *tawba* and forgiveness, with images of sweet tears and background music guiding us through the days.

Instead it is often a struggle, and hard work. Background music does not play and many a dry eye begins to wonder if this seeking of forgiveness business is even working.

Tawba is a lot like cleaning a closet. Before you start, the closet looks fine. It might not be something you would show your mother-in-law, but it does not seem to be that big of a job. Six hours into cleaning it, though, you are dusty, sweaty, and surrounded by piles. Children are beginning to fuss and whine, dinner needs to be made, and you are tempted to bag it all and try again next month.

Do not succumb!

Step by step, deal with the piles. Wash the floor, fold and hang, and put all the pieces back together. Stand back and look at your sparkling, organized closet. Now it will serve you well.

In the middle of a *tawba*, we are feeling a lot messier than we felt at the beginning of the month. Surrounded by lists of sins, shortcomings, and character flaws along with the rest of the world beckoning for attention, you may be tempted to just forget it and try again in Ramadan.

Do not succumb!

Step by step, deal with the sins, wash your heart, hone and tone your character and put yourself back together. Stand back and present your new self to the *umma* of our beloved Messenger ﷺ. Now you will be able to serve the *umma* in truly productive ways.

Are you tired? Make yourself a strong cup of coffee and hold on to *istighfār*. Let the words energize you and fill you.

Are you frustrated? Give money in charity to someone in need; give a gift card to a student; send your mother a gift box. Let the coolness of easing someone else's hardship calm you.

Are you thinking that you might not want to improve? That you are fine just the way you are? Take a chance on becoming your best self. Take a chance on becoming of the best of people ever created. Take a chance on a full *tawba*.

You are the best of peoples brought forth for humanity, enjoining what is right and preventing what is wrong and believing in God.. (3:110)

كُنتُمْ خَيْرَ أُمَّةٍ أُخْرِجَتْ لِلنَّاسِ تَأْمُرُونَ بِٱلْمَعْرُوفِ وَتَنْهَوْنَ عَنِ ٱلْمُنكَرِ وَتُؤْمِنُونَ بِٱللَّهِ

Only through *tawba* can we hope to become the *umma* that we were meant to be. Enjoin what is right within your very self. Prevent evil and wrongdoing in your intentions and deeds. Be encouraged – just like the closet seems worse before it becomes better, you are on your way to health and healing. Decide to make a change. Seek forgiveness for what is past. The forgiveness of Rajab is washing you, sorting you, and fixing you. Don't quit. A shining, clean and joyful heart awaits you. The *umma* awaits you.

Reflection

Why do you think forgiveness is so often tied to charity? Have you ever given charity with the intention of seeking forgiveness?

Project

If you are behind on your *istighfār*, set this week as your week to catch up! Really taste the words and feel their nourishment. If you give something in charity in the name of your *tawba*, write about it here. Do not be discouraged by the piles of outstanding sins, or even of *istighfārs* you have not yet done.. Keep going! You will get there, insha'Allah, and your bright, clean heart will thank you.

Reflection / Project

Week 31

Bankrupt?

ABŪ HURAIRA 🙵 REPORTS that the Prophet 🙵 said, "Do you know who is bankrupt?"

The companions answered, "The bankrupt one among us, O Messenger of God, is he who has not a dirham, nor belongings."

He 🙵 said, "The bankrupt of my nation is he who comes on the Day of Judgment with fasts, prayers and zakat, yet he comes having abused someone, slandered someone, and taken another's money. He is kept back and this one takes of his good deeds, and that one takes of his good deeds. Then if his deeds are exhausted before his offenses have been cleared, some of their sins will be taken and laid upon him. Then he will be thrown into hellfire." (*Musnad al-Imām Aḥmad*)

«إن المفلس من أمتي من يأتي يوم القيامة بصيام وصلاة وزكاة ويأتي قد شتم عرض هذا وقذف هذا وأكل مال هذا فيقعد فيقتص هذا من حسناته وهذا من حسناته فإن فنيت حسناته قبل أن يقضي ما عليه من الخطايا أخذ من خطاياهم فطرحت عليه ثم طرح في النار.»

There is a syndrome wherein, as one takes on more religiosity, she becomes short-tempered and judgmental. Her clothes may have gotten wider, but her heart has shrunken to a narrow way. His beard may be growing, but his compassion is shrinking. This is the bankrupt syndrome.

In life and finances it is easy to go bankrupt when you do not understand how much money you have, or the bills you have to pay. I remember my first pay-check at sixteen – I thought I was rich! It disappeared in a short fifteen minutes, and I quickly learned that if I was going to save money for college, I was going to have to learn to interact differently with money.

In religion, we fill our hearts with fasting, praying, and paying zakat. Sometimes that can be like a first pay-check. Having not experienced the light of guidance before, a newly practicing Muslim can think she is rich in righteousness. This can translate into self-righteousness, arrogance and judgmental behavior, which lead to generally poor behavior and then bankruptcy in the next world.

It is very easy to point out the faults in others, to see how others have shortchanged us and to feel slighted. It is more difficult to recognize our own faults, to see how others view us and to recognize the pain we may be causing other people.

In order to protect our investment, we must learn to be people of the best behavior. We need to be living, breathing shelters for each other. We need to hold ourselves to great heights, and be gently accepting of each other's states.

The Prophet ﷺ was an example of excellent behavior. He was helpful in the house, he would pause to speak to children and the elderly, he was patient with poor behavior. Once, a bedoiun came into the Prophet's mosque in Medina. He grabbed the Prophet ﷺ by his shirt such that the edge of it dug into his neck. The other companions – and especially ʿUmar 🅐 – went for their swords, but the Prophet 🅐 indicated that they should leave him be. The bedoiun asked the Prophet 🅐 in short, brusque words about his identity, his prophethood, and the rules of Islam. The Prophet 🅐 answered him calmly, politely, and fully. The man entered Islam.

Another time a man urinated in the mosque. The Prophet 🅐 showed incredible tolerance as he kept back the wrath of the other companions while gently directing the man in how to clean up his 'mess'.

Protect yourself from bankruptcy with excellent behavior.

Be a pleasant and forgiving person. When you are pleasant you run less risk of hurting others. Smile at people (it counts as charity – you can rack up some good deeds while avoiding people's heavy hearts).

Make it a point to be well-behaved wherever you go, amongst Muslims and amongst non-Muslims. Be polite, greet people, be agreeable.

Of the most important behavior is that rendered to those closest to us. Be loving and forgiving – leave your *nafs* behind – when dealing with parents, in-laws and husbands, siblings, friends, and coworkers. Give people excuses – as Imām al-Ghazālī recommends, "Give your brother who has wronged you seventy excuses, and if you find naught, look for another."

Avoid argument. Bickering and whining, complaining and loud sighing are all poor manners, along with rolling of the eyes and mean sarcasm.

Practice daily acts of kindness. Avoid hurtful behavior. Bring joy to others. Avoid hurting anyone.

As we work to increase our prayers, prepare for Ramadan, and investigate what we owe in zakat this year, let us remember that the richness of our faith is shown in our interactions with others. Let our behavior be of gold, precious stones, and billion-dollar investments, and let us never be of those who are bankrupt in any way, in this life or the next.

Reflection

Think about how many times you smiled at others this week. How many times did you hold a door open or greet someone coming the other way? Sometimes we fall into a self-absorbed phase and lose touch with others. Are you projecting an open, kind, positive image to everyone you meet?

Project

Think of a person you have a problem with. Sit down and literally write seventy excuses for the behaviors that you do not like. Literally. Seventy. If you get stuck and cannot think of an excuse, write something that that person has done for you. See how you feel about them at the end of the exercise. How do you feel at the end of this activity about the whole enterprise of assigning blame and holding grudges?

Reflection / Project

Week 32

The Opportunity: Niṣf Shaʿbān

SHE WALKS QUIETLY TO her kitchen and pulls out the coffee maker. As the rich smell of caffeine confuses the usual nighttime smells, she pulls out her prayer carpet and her expensive perfume. The night awaits her and she is seeking forgiveness and the pleasure of her Lord.

It is Niṣf Shaʿbān.

An argument on Facebook and comments on Twitter run through her mind and she shakes her head and thinks of ʿĀʾisha 🌸, who, when she asked the Prophet 🌸 about his long prostration (indeed she had feared the worst!), was told, "Do you know what night this is?... This is the Night of Mid-Shaʿbān. God looks at His servants on the night of Mid-Shaʿbān and forgives those seeking forgiveness, has mercy on those seeking mercy, and leaves the bearers of grudges as they are." (al-Bayhaqī)

»هذه ليلة النصف من شعبان، إن الله يطلع على عباده في ليلة النصف من شعبان فيغفر للمستغفرين ويرحم المسترحمين، ويؤخر أهل الحقد كما هم.«

She thinks of Ali 🌸, who tells us that the Prophet 🌸 said, "If it is the night of Mid-Shaʿbān, then stand (in

159

prayer) in its night and fast its day. For God descends to the heavens of the earth when the sun sets and says, 'Is there anyone who seeks forgiveness so that I may forgive him? Is there anyone who seeks provision so that I may grant him provision? Is there anyone afflicted so that I may remove his affliction? Is there not such and such...' until the break of dawn." (*Sunan Ibn Māja*)

»إذا كانت ليلة النصف من شعبان، فقوموا ليلها وصوموا نهارها. فإن الله ينزل فيها لغروب الشمس إلى سماء الدنيا. فيقول: ألا من مستغفر لي فأغفر له! ألا من مسترزق فأرزقه! ألا مبتلى فأعافيه! ألا كذا ألا كذا، حتى يطلع الفجر.«

She remembers the advice of al-Subkī, the great *mufassir* of Quran, who said that the night of Mid-Shaʿbān atones for the sins of a year, the night of Friday atones for the sins of the week, and the Night of Power (Lailat al-Qadr) atones for the sins of a lifetime.

She turns off her computer, switches off her phone, pours her coffee and dons her freshly ironed prayer clothes.

The night has begun and she does not want to be left behind.

Islam is a religion of opportunity, and the night of the fifteenth of Shaʿbān is one of those opportunities. Fifteen days before Ramadan, it is a chance to stand in the downpouring rain of Allah's mercy and shed our sins one by one as we stand in prayer and the remembrance of God.

The one deprived of this opportunity has been described by the early scholars as the miserable one. According to ʿĀʾisha, ﷺ The Prophet ﷺ said, "Jibrīl has come to me and said, 'This is the night of Niṣf Shaʿbān. By God, the number of people who will be saved from the Fire in it are as the number of hairs on the sheep of [the tribe] of Kalb.

In it God will not look at a polytheist, one who incites rancor in the hearts of people towards others, one who severs the bonds of kinship, one who drags his clothing (is haughty), one who transgresses against his parents, or one who is addicted to alcohol.'" (*Kanz al-ʿUmmāl*)

»بل أتاني جبريل فقال: هذه الليلة ليلة النصف من شعبان، ولله فيها عتقاء من النار بعدد شعور غنم كلب، لا ينظر الله فيها إلى مشرك ولا إلى مشاحن ولا إلى قاطع رحم ولا إلى مسبل ولا إلى عاق لوالديه ولا إلى مدمن خمر.«

While idolatry and alcohol are probably not real concerns for her, she worries about her effect on the hearts of people, her duties toward her family, and her own arrogance. So today and all of last week she has been catching up with family. She reevaluated her relationships and made sure she was not saying anything to her in-laws about her husband that might upset them, or vice-versa. She looked at her clothes, and, recognizing that pride and arrogance are no longer in clothes that drag on the floor, looked for modern signs of such in her wardrobe. She called each parent and made sure there were no pressing needs, and that they were pleased with her.

Now, tonight, she stands in hope of reward from her Lord. She calls out and asks for forgiveness. Tears stream down her face as she remembers early years of distance and sin. Her heart breaks as she remembers times she was less than kind to others.

As Fajr begins to line the night sky, her heart is full and thankful. *Allāhumma ṣalli ʿalā sayyidinā Muhammad.* She thinks of him now. And asks that prayers and blessings, equal in number to the drops of water in the sea, will be sent to him.

What a beautiful night. *Al-ḥamdu l-i-Llāh.*

Reflection

All sins, especially those of intention and attitude, exist in degrees. While we may not flaunt our designer labels, we may secretly look down upon those whose outfits don't match or whose clothes are tattered. While we don't spurn our in-laws to their faces, we may talk about them behind their backs, maybe even on social media. We may harbor bitter feelings toward them in our hearts. Niṣf Shaʿbān is a night to examine oneself deeply and closely. A night for unflinching honesty in order that true *tawba* can be made. Find your hidden arrogance or stirring up of bad feelings or whatever your personal barrier is between you and Allah. Face it. Battle it. Surrender it to Allah and make *tawba* for it. Write about it here if you wish.

Project

Plan ahead for your night of mid-Shaʿbān. Vacuum the carpet, wash and iron your prayer clothes, perfume your prayer rugs. Buy special coffee and treats. Invite your children or neighbors, friends or even online acquaintances to experience the night together. Then make *dhikr*, *duʿāʾ*, *tawba* and salat until the rise of the sun!

Reflection / Project

_____
_____
_____
_____
_____
_____
_____
_____
_____
_____
_____
_____
_____
_____
_____
_____
_____
_____
_____
_____
_____
_____
_____

Week 33

Our Statement of Faith

WHEN I VISIT ENGLAND, I see wrap scarves of various shades everywhere – long flowing scarves covered in flowers, black scarves and white scarves, striped scarves and spotted scarves. The landscape is covered with a garden of hijabi women.

In St. Paul, MN, I see a woman in a scarf manning the cash register at my local pharmacy, and our police force is the first in the nation to allow a hijabi woman to be on the force in her hijab.

On a road trip through the Midwest, I stop for gas in small town America and am greeted with *"al-salāmu ʿalaykum"* by a woman in hijab.

President Obama had a hijabi woman staged in one of his political photos, Ottawa used hijabi women to demonstrate their inclusive culture, and even the Oscars had a hijabi woman make an appearance on the red carpet in 2014.

Hijab is becoming more prevalent across the Western world, even as it becomes more controversial within our communities. We discuss the question of obligation and relevance, we are fraught with fear about worldly opportunity, and we fight the opposing needs to blend in and to fulfill the duty of hijab.

Within families, the hijab can be a point of controversy as young women put it on to their parents' chagrin or refuse to put it on to their parents' disappointment.

The hijab is a fascinating part of our faith lives. In Sūrat al-Nūr, Allah the Exalted tells the believing women to

$$وَلْيَضْرِبْنَ بِخُمُرِهِنَّ عَلَىٰ جُيُوبِهِنَّ$$

... *wrap their headscarves over their 'neck-slits'*, (24:31) (the Arabic word refers to the area of the neck and anything open of the clothing below it).

Then in Sūrat al-Aḥzāb the order is repeated when He ﷻ tells the believing women to

$$يُدْنِينَ عَلَيْهِنَّ مِن جَلَابِيبِهِنَّ$$

... *lower over themselves of their outer garments* (33:59) (including in meaning a headscarf here as well).

When the believing women of Medina heard the order to wear hijab, they immediately tore their embroidered fabric from the bottoms of their dresses and used it to fulfill the conditions of hijab.

The hijab is the ultimate feminist statement. It says, 'This body is mine. I choose who looks at it.'

The hijab is a loud statement of affiliation. It is a team T-shirt that says, "I am a Muslim woman!" It is a social consciousness and a spiritual stance.

Hijab is one of the most powerful symbols of identity known to the world – and it is worn by women alone.

Hijab is the beginning of obedience on this path. To submit to God alone, not to society or men, not to family or philosophy, not to personal whim or desire, is to begin the path of faith with strong legs and long steps. It is to live every day as a day of racked up reward. It is to live in the shelter of the Quranic injunction. To wear hijab is to wear our religion.

As more and more women wear hijab, we begin to change the fabric and expectations of society. We make it easier for the next woman who wishes to walk the path of divine obedience. We become a force to be reckoned with.

Let us tie our scarves with a smile today and step with strength upon the sidewalks of the various places we live. Our very presence is a reminder to others that this religion will not go away. That the followers of Muhammad ﷺ will emulate him. That the worship of the One God will not disappear from the earth. *Allāhu Akbar.*

Reflections

Tawakkol Karman is the first Arab woman and youngest winner of the Nobel Peace Prize. The Muslim Times reports, "When asked about her hijab by journalists and how it is not proportionate with her level of intellect and education, she replied, 'Man in the early times was almost naked, and as his intellect evolved he started wearing clothes. What I am today and what I'm wearing represents the highest level of thought and civilization that man has achieved, and is not regressive. It's the removal of clothes again that is regressive back to ancient times.'"

Reflect on your own responses to questions about hijab. Think about how you might reply in the future.

Project

Go out this week and buy yourself a new scarf! If you can afford it, get one for a friend as well. Do this even if you do not currently wear hijab! Buy a scarf and try it on; experiment with different ways of tying it and see how the colors match with your clothes. As you are doing that, pay attention to how it makes you feel and where those feelings might be coming from. Have you fallen victim to the culture of desireability? Are you afraid of looking "backward", and as a result are letting others define "forward" for you?

Reflection / Project

Week 34

A Letter from a Friend

ear Friends,

It has been a year since we last met. I hope you have been well. I will be arriving in a few days, and I'm wondering if you are ready...

Are you ready for me? I am waiting for your voice – looking forward to hearing it as it ripples sound waves of Quran over and through my minutes and seconds.

Are you ready for me? I am waiting for your longing – looking forward to responding to your beating heart with my gifts.

Are you ready for me? I am waiting for your charity – looking forward to the smiles of all who receive of your generosity.

Are you ready for me? I am waiting for your prayers – looking forward to supporting you in long minutes of standing, bowing, and pleading with your Lord.

Are you ready for me? I am waiting for your tears – looking forward to each splash of *tawba* as it mixes with the fibers of hope that I provide.

As usual, I have packed in the corners of my bags some special treats, just for you.

During the first ten days of my visit, I will present to you

169

a daily gift of mercy. Mercy is what you have when you deal gently with an employee who is insubordinate, mercy is what you show when you ignore your child's carelessness in chores, and mercy is what you hope for when you crash the brand new car. I do not bring you the mercy of humanity, however: I bring you Allah's mercy. I bring you the overlooking of your sins...Every single day I will offer it to you and hope that you take it from my outstretched hand...

In the second ten days of my visit, I will have a new gift: the gift of forgiveness. You will find that these days are a little more difficult than the previous ones – but do not give up! Forgiveness! On any one of these days you could be forgiven for all your past sins. Forgiveness. Could your book be wiped clean? Yes! For that is what forgiveness is. Every day of the second ten days I will place a beautifully wrapped box on the shelf. You have only to call out for it in repentance and it will be yours.

Finally, on the last ten days, I will have the greatest gift of all: freedom from hellfire. How, you might ask, can I offer such a gift? I offer you great and deep change. When you change in such a way, you remove the chains that are chaining you to hellfire. If you accept this gift from me, you will have changed deeply – you will have turned away from your past sins and bad habits and begun to carve out a new future – a future that has no fear of hellfire, and hopes for paradise and the pleasure of your Lord.

I have missed you so much. All these long months I thought about you, and remembered how we spent the time together last year. I remember a little too much time spent sleeping, a few too many hours in the kitchen, and not quite enough Quran. A couple of times you missed *tahajjud*, and once you missed *tarāwīḥ*. Still, last year was better than the previous year...we won't even talk about that.

I have great hopes for us this year. I am imagining us together – hand in hand all month, with Angel Jibrīl himself shaking your hand in congratulations at the Eid prayer.

Before I arrive, let us make a schedule, a plan. How many times do you plan to complete the reading of the Quran this month, and how many *rakʿas* of prayer do you plan to pray daily? How many people will you feed and how will you help those around you to benefit from me as well?

Remember, I come but once a year. Every moment and second that I am with you is important. I am on the way.

Are you ready.?

Love, Ramadan

Reflection

What do you hope to achieve from this Ramadan? Write down 3 goals – one social, one spiritual and one character related. What do you need to do to achieve these goals? Change takes time and preparation – how will you prepare to make these changes this Ramadan?

Project

Write what your ideal Ramadan *ʿibāda* schedule would look like. Examine your work schedule or your children's schedules and figure out the best way to fit your life around your extra *ʿibāda* this month. Write your schedule and plan here.

Reflection / Project

Week 35

A Quenching Cure

RAMADAN IS OUR MONTH of fasting. And while we stop food and drink from entering our mouths, we have something more delicious and more thirst-quenching to replace it. Ramadan is the month of Quran:

شَهْرُ رَمَضَانَ ٱلَّذِىٓ أُنزِلَ فِيهِ ٱلْقُرْءَانُ

The month in which the Quran was first revealed... (2:185)

Al-ḥamdu l-i-Llāh for this Book – for its words of truth and its words of light, which, when they roll on the tongue, change the very cells of our bodies. Make us more obedient, happier. Cleanse us of bitterness and pain and hurt. The words of the Quran heal us.

We are a fractured people. Our *umma* is broken and breaking; our families are living in separate rooms and living separate lives. We hurt each other's feelings and then defend ourselves for our hurtful actions. As individuals, our feelings are all over the place. We are attached to a myriad of things that are not Allah ﷻ or His prophet ﷺ or His religion. Our fractured hearts make us feel lonely and we become sensitive to people's words and actions, which only fractures us more.

The Quran can heal *all* of that. It knits our bits and pieces into a whole and cools our burning feelings. We need only to read it. And read it. And read it. It is the reading in Arabic that cures us – even if it is at a snail's pace. Reading the translation is an important aspect of understanding, but it is not the healing balm.

Our cure is the Quran.

Whatever it is that ails you – whether it is a painful back or a broken heart – the Quran carries within it healing.

It is said that Shaikh Abū al-Qāsim al-Qushayrī's son was severely ill and he said, "I despaired of him living, and it weighed heavily upon me. Then I saw the Prophet ﷺ in a dream and told him of my son. He said to me, 'Where are you and the verses of healing?' I woke and thought about it, and found six verses of healing:

$$وَيَشْفِ صُدُورَ قَوْمٍ مُّؤْمِنِينَ ﴿١٤﴾$$

…and heal the breasts of the believing people (9:14)

$$وَشِفَآءٌ لِّمَا فِى ٱلصُّدُورِ$$

…a healing for what is in the breasts (10:57)

$$يَخْرُجُ مِنۢ بُطُونِهَا شَرَابٌ مُّخْتَلِفٌ أَلْوَٰنُهُۥ فِيهِ شِفَآءٌ لِّلنَّاسِ إِنَّ فِى ذَٰلِكَ لَءَايَةً لِّقَوْمٍ يَتَفَكَّرُونَ ﴿٦٩﴾$$

…There emerges from their bellies a drink, varying in colors, in which there is healing for people. (16:69)

$$وَنُنَزِّلُ مِنَ ٱلْقُرْءَانِ مَا هُوَ شِفَآءٌ وَرَحْمَةٌ لِّلْمُؤْمِنِينَ$$

174

...And We send down of the Quran that which is healing and mercy for the believers (17:82)

وَإِذَا مَرِضْتُ فَهُوَ يَشْفِينِ ۝

And when I am ill, it is He who cures me (26:80)

قُلْ هُوَ لِلَّذِينَ ءَامَنُواْ هُدَى وَشِفَآءٌ

Say, «It is, for those who believe, a guidance and cure.» (41:44)

He continues, "So I wrote them on a paper and soaked them in water, then gave it to him to drink and it was as though he was released from his illness."

Meditate for a moment on the fact that this book of words contains the words of God, of Allah, of the Creator. The One who made the mountains spoke these words. The One who created the giraffe spoke these words. The One who created trees that sprout purple and green leaves spoke these words. The One; Allah the One; the Quran is the Words of God Almighty.

Read the Quran. Let the Arabic words flow over your tongue and heart. If your tongue stumbles, then know you have more reward and do not allow difficulty to pull you away. Let your tongue roll over the letters. When it is easy, you get seventy times the reward for each letter (now in Ramadan). When it is difficult, you get double that. As the Prophet ﷺ tells us,

«الماهر بالقرآن مع السفرة الكرام البررة، والذي يقرأ القرآن ويتتعتع فيه، وهو عليه شاق، له أجران.»

"The one who is proficient in Quran is with the scribe, noble, devout angels. And the one who reads the Quran and stammers in it, finding difficulty therein, receives a doubled reward." (*Ṣaḥīḥ Muslim*)

The raining reward washes us as much as the words themselves.

We are in an era of the Olympics, celebrity chefs and higher degrees. We are a generation of super-moms with high-powered jobs. We are a generation that recognizes that hard work determines success.

Let us take the energy that bubbles below the culture and apply it to our *dīn*. Let us pour ourselves into the Quran. In the recitation and memorization of the words of God is a healing for our tired hearts and disappointed hopes.

Let us be cured – in our hearts and our lives, let the Quran cure our families and our neighborhoods. Let our reading of the Quran spread out and blanket the *umma* of our beloved Prophet ﷺ with the cure for what ails us.

In this month of fasting, let us feast upon the words of Allah the Exalted.

Your cure, my cure, our cure... The Quran.

Reflection

What do you need to be cured of? What is there in your heart that needs healing? What has been sitting on your heart, worrying you, that you can hand over to Allah this month? Does your body need healing as well? List the things you want to ask healing of – and come back and add to the list as Ramadan goes on.

Project

Decide how many chapters, portions (*ajzā'*) or complete readings of the Quran (*khitmas*) you want to finish this Ramadan. Do not let anyone tell you that if you canot read perfectly you should not read at all. There is no other way to improve. If you do not know Arabic at all, listen to the Quran and make a goal of learning your Arabic letters this month. Whatever goal you choose, make it your number one Ramadan priority.

Tip

One secret to meeting these goals is to do the math. Sit down and divide out your goal. You want to finish Sūrat al-Baqara? It has 48 pages. Divided by 29 days that is just over 1.5 pages per day. Dedicate a specific time each day to Quran reading, and make the time sacred, not allowing anything else to creep in and impose on it.

Reflection / Project

_____

_____

_____

_____

_____

_____

_____

_____

_____

_____

_____

_____

_____

_____

_____

_____

_____

_____

_____

_____

_____

Week 36

Ramadan Rulings

FTER ELEVEN MONTHS DEDICATED to our bodies, Ramadan arrives for our spirits. It is a month filled with spiritual possibilities, and each person will benefit based on her commitment to her religion, her understanding of the rulings of Ramadan, and the effort she puts into the rites of Ramadan.

Allah ﷻ says in the Quran,

$$شَهْرُ رَمَضَانَ ٱلَّذِىٓ أُنزِلَ فِيهِ ٱلْقُرْءَانُ هُدًى لِّلنَّاسِ وَبَيِّنَـٰتٍ مِّنَ ٱلْهُدَىٰ وَٱلْفُرْقَانِ فَمَن شَهِدَ مِنكُمُ ٱلشَّهْرَ فَلْيَصُمْهُ$$

"The month of Ramadan [is that] in which was revealed the Quran, a guidance for the people and clear proofs of guidance and criterion. So whoever is present during the month, let him fast it." (2:185)

The fast of Ramadan is a pillar of faith. Ibn Umar ﷺ narrates that the Messenger of God said, "Islam is built upon five: Testifying that there is no god but Allah and that Muhammad is the Messenger of Allah, performing the prayer, giving zakat, performing hajj, and fasting Ramadan." (*Ṣaḥīḥ al-Bukhārī*)

«بُنِي الإسلامُ على خمسٍ: شهادةِ أن لا إله إلا الله
وأن محمدا رسول الله، وإقام الصلاة، وإيتاء الزكاة،
والحج، وصوم رمضان.»

It is a serious matter, and the scholars have agreed that the one who does not fast, without any excuse, enters into the dangerous world of disbelief. There are valid reasons not to fast: chronic illness or serious illness wherein fasting would worsen the illness, travel and a child who has not reached puberty (the fast of a child who is old enough to make a decision about fasting is accepted and rewarded, but she is not obliged to fast until puberty).

In general, however, fasting is an obligation upon every one of us. The Western misconception that pregnancy and nursing automatically offer a 'get out of fasting' card is dangerous to our spiritual development.

Pregnancy and nursing each have their own rulings, and each depends greatly on the health of the mother, the health of the child, and a number of other variables. In general, however, pregnant and nursing mothers should start the day fasting – intending to fast – and then if it becomes too difficult, so much so that harm may come to the child or herself, she may break her fast. The fast will have to be made up, of course, and there are a few other rules to be taken into account regarding that. A pregnant or nursing mother who fears for her child or herself should work with a practicing Muslim doctor who understands the spiritual enormity of fasting, as well as the obvious need to protect the physical health of mother and child.

We are responsible for our unborn child and for ourselves. As Muslims, we understand that the responsibility manifests itself both physically and spiritually. When I was nursing my firstborn, many women of the community discouraged me and tried to shame me into breaking my fast. Thankfully, I did not, and I had more milk that month than any other month before or since. I am not implying that it will work for every mother, but I was a young and healthy woman. There was no reason for me not to try and fast, and the blessing of Ramadan manifested itself greatly.

In order for our fast to be valid and fulfill the conditions of fasting, we must make the intention to fast and we must abstain from food, drink and sexual activity.

Recommended and rewarded deeds of Ramadan fasting include: hastening the breaking of the fast, to break one's fast with dates, to make *du'ā'* (pray) when breaking the fast because the *du'ā'* of a fasting person is answered; to have *suḥūr* (the predawn breakfast), to read extra Quran, give extra money in charity, break the fasts of our brothers and sisters in faith, and participate in *i'tikāf* (seclusion for worship in the last days).

Deeds that are *makrūh* (disliked/disdained) for a fasting person include: cursing, quarreling and insults, looking at that which will tempt you to break your fast, putting anything in the mouth that might result in accidental swallowing, and intentionally delaying the breaking of the fast.

The rulings of Ramadan are straightforward and easy to understand. Each Muslim should review the rulings of her *madhhab* to ensure that she is reaping as much reward as possible.

It is one month. The days pass by quickly. One month for the spirit. One month to put aside our bodily cravings and focus instead on our spiritual nutrition. May we be of those who leave the month of Ramadan with rosy-cheeked and chubby-legged spirits, that we may live on that sustenance for the rest of the year.

Reflection

Which *sunnas* have you generally always fulfilled during Ramadan? Which new ones can you add this year? Pick one or two and schedule them in!

Project

One of the most difficult and rewarding parts of fasting is standing special guard over our tongues. This includes avoiding backbiting, of course, but it also includes snapping at children, arguing with husbands and indulging in negative self-talk. We stand a much better chance of success in training our tongues if we devise a battle plan. Make a training strategy! Choose some redirecting methods for when you feel yourself slipping into dangerous "talkitory" (like specific *dhikr* you will make instead, for example) and consequences to fulfill if you fall completely off the wagon. Find yourself being snarky or shouting at your children or siblings? Give a set extra amount in charity or offer a set number of *rakʿas* in *tawba*. Write your plan here and commit to soaking up every bit of Allah's mercy possible this month!

Reflection / Project

Week 37

Finding My Badr

ON THE SEVENTEENTH OF Ramadan, in the second year after the *hijra*, the fledgling Muslim army faced the large and experienced army of the Quraish. They stood against impossible odds, ridiculously outnumbered and outmaneuvered. The fight began with a series of one-on-one duels, continued with a great battle into which angels descended as fighters, and ended with the Muslims victorious.

The Battle of Badr was a pivotal moment in our history. The Muslims who went forth to Badr went forth into the unknown. Unlike later battles, where the Muslims would be required to participate, Badr was voluntary. It was an act of pure devotion and commitment. It was the fulfillment of an earlier oath and a demonstration of love.

Much later, one of the soldiers of Badr will commit a grave error against the state, and 'Umar ﷺ will ask to be allowed to execute him. The Prophet ﷺ will say, "He was present at Badr, and you do not know, perhaps Allah looked upon the people of Badr and said: 'Do what you wish, for I have forgiven you.'" (*Bukhāri and Muslim*)

«إنه قد شهد بدرا، وما يدريك لعل الله أن يكون قد اطلع على أهل بدر فقال: اعملوا ما شئتم فقد غفرت لكم.»

Scholars have struggled with this hadith. Forgiven? What does that mean? How can it be? And as a result have come forth with a number of theories about the 'actual' meaning of the hadith versus the 'allegorical' meaning. For me, however, the hadith is not confusing. Badr was a great and glorious deed.

It was labor and delivery.

It was the offering of a kidney.

It was the jumping into a frozen river to pull out a toddler.

Badr was that which renders all minor mistakes void. If you are carrying your sister's kidney, you will forgive her for forgetting your birthday. If your toddler's savior is coldly unwelcoming, you will not hold a grudge. It is difficult to be consistently good to our mothers because we do not remember their sacrifices, but once a woman becomes a mother herself, she becomes much more forgiving of her mother's irritating quirks.

Badr.

What deed will we do for Islam that could possibly be our Badr? How can we sacrifice, give, and support Islam as the early companions did? What great and glorious deed can we do for this *dīn*?

Badr was about carrying and defending the *umma*. It was about making sure that Islam had a chance to be established on the earth.

How are we carrying and defending our *umma*? Our communities? It is not enough to just selfishly take care of ourselves. We must make time for others. We must make time to join the movement to establish Islam as a healthy and viable option for the spiritually thirsty and morally desperate. We must stand up and carry the standard of Islam and look for a place in the 'frontlines'.

As we look to our *umma*, do we see any 'Badrs'? Do we see great and glorious deeds that are meant to support our *umma* and establish Islam on the earth? I believe we do. We do not have to build our own Badr, but we can join a Badr already in progress. Look to the projects that need volunteers and volunteer your time. Learn to organize and prioritize your life so that it is more than just the daily grind. Islam is our priority – in our personal lives, in our family lives and in our wider communities.

Find your Badr. Find the great and glorious deed that will protect you from your own future mistakes. Find a way to be of those about whom Allah ﷻ might say, 'do as you wish, for I have forgiven you.'

Reflection

One of the members of the army at Badr – a cousin of Abū Bakr's ﵁ named Misṭaḥ – would later fall victim to participating in the slander against ʿĀʾisha ﵂. Abū Bakr had been in the habit of helping to support Misṭaḥ because he was poor. When he heard that his cousin had slandered his own daughter, he vowed never to give him charity again, but Allah revealed this *āya*:

$$وَلَا يَأْتَلِ أُوْلُواْ ٱلْفَضْلِ مِنكُمْ وَٱلسَّعَةِ أَن يُؤْتُواْ أُوْلِى ٱلْقُرْبَىٰ وَٱلْمَسَـٰكِينَ وَٱلْمُهَـٰجِرِينَ فِى سَبِيلِ ٱللَّهِ وَلْيَعْفُواْ وَلْيَصْفَحُوٓاْ أَلَا تُحِبُّونَ أَن يَغْفِرَ ٱللَّهُ لَكُمْ وَٱللَّهُ غَفُورٌ رَّحِيمٌ ۝$$

And let not those of virtue among you and wealth swear not to give [aid] to their relatives and the needy and the emigrants for the cause of Allah, and let them pardon and overlook. Would you not like that Allah should forgive you? And Allah is Forgiving and Merciful. (24:22).

Is there someone in your life who is a relative, and/or who has done a Badr type thing for you, yet whom you hold stubbornly to account for their shortcomings? What is causing you to withhold your forgiveness? Can you come to a place where you are able to forgive them?

Project

Choose a Badr type project for yourself. Is there something you have always wanted to do for Islam, but have felt that you did not have the time or the resources? Make the time and reach out for the resources! Those who went out at Badr gave their all and were assisted by angels as reinforcements. Do not think that those angels are retired! They are still sent by Allah to help those struggling in His cause! Step out in faith and in the full knowledge that during this sacred month Allah will shower His blessings and energy upon you, and begin your Badr today.

Reflection / Project

Week 38

The Final Paper and Exam

THE MONTH OF RAMADAN is a course, and each day is its own lesson. One by one the days come and go, honing us and toning us and turning us into people of *taqwā*.

يَـٰٓأَيُّهَا ٱلَّذِينَ ءَامَنُوا۟ كُتِبَ عَلَيْكُمُ ٱلصِّيَامُ كَمَا كُتِبَ عَلَى ٱلَّذِينَ مِن قَبْلِكُمْ لَعَلَّكُمْ تَتَّقُونَ ۝

O you who believe, fasting has been prescribed for you as it was prescribed for those before you, that you may have taqwā. (2:183)

The end of Ramadan offers new tools for growth. It offers new opportunities to better our souls. We have been fasting and developing *taqwā*, reading Quran and filling our hearts with guidance, and standing in *tarāwīḥ*, bringing delight to our souls. Now we have the opportunity for self-discovery. The *sunna* of *iʿtikāf* is upon us. Here we fast, pray, read Quran, and face our demons. It is the decision to spend days or weeks in reflection and worship away from the distraction of this world and inside the mosque.

Women are uniquely blessed in this area, for all we need to do is declare our home, or a place in our home, 'our masjid' and then intend *iʿtikāf* within it:

189

«هذا مسجدي ونويت الاعتكاف فيه.»

"This is my mosque and I intend *i'tikāf* in it."

We then fill our time with activities that befit a masjid: Quran reading, praying, reflecting and remembering God.

By now, some of the enthusiasm of the beginning of Ramadan may be waning. The real world may be getting to you. Exhaustion may be setting in... Intend *i'tikāf* in your home. Then live the next days as though you are in a mosque. This does not preclude the household chores, but it does mean rushing to finish them to get back to your Quran, your remembrance, your reflection. It is a time when that which needs fixing will come to mind. Do not brush the realization away like an annoying fly, but push the pause button and face it. Use the fasting, Quran reading and all night praying to help you overcome your weaknesses and shortcomings, and to bring you to a place of *tawba*.

I'tikāf can be done for one hour or one day or longer. It is a simple intention followed up by a seriousness of attitude and action. Now, in our homes, let us say, "This is my mosque" and let us intend *i'tikāf*. It is an additional *sunna* that will take us to that place of cure that we all seek.

As we spend time in *i'tikāf*, we are looking for the most important night of the year, Lailat al-Qadr. This is a night of answered prayer, peace and great closeness to Allah ﷻ.

Indeed, We sent the Quran down during the night of Power/ and what can make you know what is the Night of Power/ The Night of Power is better than a thousand months/ The angels and Spirit descend therein by permission of their Lord for every matter/ Peace it is until the emergence of dawn. (97:1-5)

A night of angels and peace, a night that is better than 1000 months (83 years!) of worship, a night of great opportunity awaits us in these last days.

We are asked to look for this night in the odd nights of the last ten days.

I find it significant that the reason we don't know the exact night of Lailat al-Qadr is because of the ill words of some men around the Prophet ﷺ. In Ṣaḥīḥ al-Bukhārī it is reported that the Prophet ﷺ came out to inform the companions of the night of Lailat al-Qadr, when two men began to argue or insult each other and so the knowledge was lifted.

This shows us that spiritual blessings are connected to behavior. Poor behavior can be the catalyst to the loss of blessings.

Now, at the end of Ramadan, we are tired, lacking sleep, food and drink. It is during this time that our *nafs* may rear its ugly head and begin to bark at the people around us: children, husbands, siblings, parents. And only Allah knows what blessings will leave with those words.

Instead, let us watch our words and behavior very carefully. When we say, "This is my mosque" and turn our homes into places of angels and peace, let that be the determiner, not only for intense worship, but exquisite behavior.

In these last ten days, as we seek powerful experiences and closeness to Allah ﷻ, let us watch our words and behavior very carefully.

Ramadan will not graduate us unless our homework and our papers and our tests are all complete.

If fasting, Quran reading, *tarāwīḥ* and generosity are the homework assignments, then *iʿtikāf* is the paper and Lailat al-Qadr is the test. The examination room is found on a secret night. It must be sought with excellent behavior and sound intention.

May Allah make us all of those who pass this course of Ramadan with top grades and honors. May Allah bless us all. *Āmīn*.

Reflection

Revisit the Ramadan goals you wrote earlier. How are you doing as far as reaching them? Write each goal here and note how close you are to achieving it. Then take advantage of these last ten days to redouble your efforts and meet those goals!

Project

Create a place in your home as your prayer space. Even if it is just a corner, place a prayer rug there and maybe a little chair and a Quran stand (this can be a little wooden one or a music stand or even just a little table). Clean it and invite the angels in with nice scents. Declare this your masjid and make *iʿtikāf* there in these last ten days of Ramadan, even if it is just a couple of hours a day or partial nights or over the weekend.

Reflection / Project

Week 39

Colorful Celebrations

T HERE IS A STREET in Mīdān, a suburb of Damascus, that is teeming with people all through the nights of Ramadan, especially toward the very end of the month. From stall to stall, people eye the nut pastries, the cheese pastries and the cream pastries. They pull out handfuls from the barrels of hard candy, chewy candy and candied fruit that line the crowded pathway. They choose chocolate bites and nougat pieces to fill their candy dishes at home.

In 2011, on the night before Eid, I stood watching all those sweet rewards as they were snatched up by procrastinating mothers and fathers from all over Damascus.

Today, many miles away in Minnesota, I prepare my home the best I can, wrap gifts in bright paper, bake sweet-smelling cinnamon treats, and attempt to create a feeling of busy excitement for my family and visitors. After the house is ready, I pull out my prayer carpet. It is time for the night of reward.

The night before Eid is called 'the night of reward', and it is said that the same number of people are released from hellfire on that night as are released in the entire month of Ramadan. And it is recorded by Ibn Māja that the Prophet ﷺ said, "Whoever spends the nights of Eid al-Fiṭr and Eid al-Aḍḥā doing righteous deeds, his heart will not die on the day when hearts die." (*Majmaʿ al-Zawāʾid*)

«من أحيا ليلة الفطر وليلة الأضحى لم يمت قلبه يوم
تموت القلوب.»

This night of reward builds anticipation for the Eid prayer. It is a night filled with the bright colors of a month well spent. As each *rakʿa* is prayed, the rainbow of reward is splayed before you. As eyes become heavy with sleep, the taste of faith awakens you. The morning comes quickly, but without *suhūr* to rustle together, it enters with a quietude and calmness that is the prequel to the rush of Eid morning.

On time for Eid prayer (hurray!) and on my right are two American convert friends, on my left an elderly Somali woman, in front of me a Pakistani woman, down a little further are some Malaysian women, and the room is salt and peppered with Egyptians, Palestinians and Syrians. . .

It is Eid.

Our holiday is a holiday of deepening joy. It begins with giving. The original *sunna* is to hand a measure of food to someone in need, which nowadays has translated to filling a box with cash at the masjid. This is Zakāt al-Fiṭr. *Al-ḥamdu l-i-Llāh!* We walk towards prayer knowing that it needs to be done before the first *takbīr*.

Then the prayer. . . What an exciting prayer! First we all sit and sing or chant the Eid *takbīr*. . . At the mosque I am at this morning, people of different nationalities keep taking the lead, so at times the tune is closer to what I have been used to (from Arab lands) and at other times the tune holds African intonations that are unfamiliar to me. It is gorgeous.

Then we stand to pray and, after shuffling purses and a rebellious car seat, we are standing shoulder to shoulder and – lo and behold – with enough room for *sujūd* in front of us. The Imam calls out 'Allāhu Akbar' and the prayer begins. There is an immediate hush upon the chatty and cheerful attendants. I hear a lone baby fussing in the other room. The imam calls out again '*Allāhu Akbar*' – which he will repeat seven times for this prayer that insists, declares, and proclaims the greatness of God Almighty. He is Great. He is Generous. He is the Lord of Ramadan and the Giver of blessings. Eyes fill with tears and hearts soften as the reward of Ramadan descends upon us.

When the prayer is over, smiling faces greet one another and the imam tries to quiet us down to tell us his *khuṭba* message. Finally we settle down and he begins. He is an immigrant -Egyptian- and I hear the Arabic in his English. It makes me smile a warm smile. Towards the end, while my heart is overflowing with love for my Muslim people, he says, "Let us pray." My head snaps up to make sure I am in the right place. A phrase I have not heard since my church days, I smile and wonder if any other convert in the room has caught that. I know for certain the imam has no idea that he has just borrowed a phrase said at every Lutheran Sunday service. The prayer (*duʿāʾ*) is short and suddenly everyone is up and laughing and hugging and talking and walking all at once.

I go with the crowd outside, manage to grab my shoes, and stop on the grass. We stand in circles, chatting with one another as family members find family members. New clothes walk past me, little girls in lemon yellow dresses, and elderly women in golden bangles, men in suits and young boys in long *dishdāshas*.

It is Eid and we are blessed.

Reflection

Look back on Eids throughout your life – did your family have any Eid traditions? Which ones brought you the most joy? What traditions might you add to make Eid a more enjoyable experience for you and your family? If this is your first Eid, what traditions did you enjoy from celebrations before you became Muslim? Can you bring them into your new Islamic life?

Project

On Eid there are always people who are left out. Students, new converts, an elderly person in a nursing home... Be on the lookout for them! Try to connect with one lonely person this Eid – you could take them cookies, plan an activity and invite them specifically or arrange to meet them at the Eid prayer. Write about how it went and include other ideas for reaching out to new people next Eid. This is how we build Islamic communities and begin to live in the shelter of each other.

Reflection / Project

Week 40

The Fasting of Shawwāl

OW THAT THE EID cookies are mere crumbs and we have caught up on our sleep, we look to begin the fasting of Shawwāl. The Prophet ﷺ said, "Whoever fasts Ramadan and six days of Shawwāl, it as though he fasted the whole year." (*Musnad al-Imām Ahmad*)

«من صام رمضان وستّا من شوال فكأنما صام السنة كلها.»

If we look at the hadith mathematically and keep in mind that deeds are multiplied ten-fold, we see that:
Ramadan multiplied by 10 = 10 months
6 days of Shawwāl multiplied by 10 = 60 days = 2 months
Together this equals 12 months, or an entire year, as the Prophet ﷺ said. It is a blessed and generous reward. May we all be able to reach it!

For women who have 7-15 days of *fard* fasting to make up, the additional six days can seem daunting, especially since there will be a portion of Shawwāl that cannot be fasted. Hence the questions begin:

- "Can I do my *sunna* fasts before my *fard* fasts?"
- "Can I combine my intention to fast my *qadā'* (make up) *fard* days with the intention of the *sunna* of Shawwāl?"

The simple answer to the second question is that the majority of scholars in this case do not permit the combination of two intentions, however – as in everything in Islam – there is much ease found in the law if we look to various opinions.

According to the Ḥanafī and Mālikī schools of thought, whoever fasts six days of Shawwāl gains the reward of fasting these voluntary fasts, whether they fast them before or after the qaḍāʾ fasts of Ramadan.

They have understood the hadith of the Prophet ﷺ simply as encouragement in hastening to voluntary fasts, whether in Shawwāl or at other times. They have interpreted the intention of the hadith as not to restrict the voluntary fasts to Shawwāl, rather that voluntary fasts are possible in any month (the important thing is the fasting of the month of Ramadan plus six [extra] days).

In the Shāfiʿī and Ḥanbali schools it is compulsory to make up all fasts owing from Ramadan first, and then to fast the six days of Shawwāl in the month of Shawwāl specifically, according to that which is mentioned in the hadith (since the hadith mentions the month of Shawwāl specifically). Here there is also emphasis on the idea that the Ramadan fasts must be complete before moving on to the reward of the six days of Shawwāl.

Focusing on the qaḍāʾ fasts could mean that some women would miss out on even one day of Shawwāl *sunna* fasting. So, if one fasts her qaḍāʾ in Shawwāl (as opposed to delaying it) in order to gain the reward of fasting in the month of Shawwāl, does she indeed gain this reward? Al-Ramlī of the Shāfiʿī school was asked whether a person who had fasts owing from Ramadan and made them up in Shawwāl had fulfilled the qaḍāʾ of Ramadan and gained the reward of the six days of Shawwāl. He answered that he had fulfilled his qaḍāʾ and had gained the reward of the six days of Shawwāl. (*Fatāwā al-Ramlī*) This is not a combining of intention. One does not say, "I intend to fast my qada prayers from Ramadan and a day of *sunna* from Shawwāl." This combined intention is what the majority of scholars disapprove of. Islam encourages crispness in our intention. It encourages clarity in our deeds. So here she is intending to make up her *qaḍāʾ* fasts first, in keeping with her school of thought, but she is doing them in the month of Shawwāl, rather than delaying them, because it is a blessed month for fasting and the Prophet 🌸 encouraged us to fast six days of the month.

Thus whatever school of thought you follow, fasting in Shawwāl is both important and greatly rewarded. May we be of those whom the Prophet 🌸 referred to as having the reward of a full year of fasting. *Āmīn.*

Reflection

As a review of your experience of Ramadan and as motivation to continue fasting in the month of Shawwāl, write some of the blessings you felt acutely during your Ramadan fasts. Insights you gained, things you realized about yourself or others, or strengths that you had not imagined you possessed.

Project

After completing the month of Ramadan, especially in summer, it is easy to let the fasts of Shawwāl go. Make a plan for your Shawwāl and *qaḍāʾ* fasts and write it here. Share your plan with friends and form a team of sisters pursuing the finish line of twelve months' fasting credit together!

Reflection / Project

_____

_____

_____

_____

_____

_____

_____

_____

_____

_____

_____

_____

_____

_____

_____

_____

_____

_____

_____

_____

_____

_____

Week 41

Avoiding the Mud

WALKING IN THE WORLD is a bit like walking in pouring rain at a campsite. The *dunyā* splashes back at us with desire, temptation, and bad habits. Just by living in the world, we are subject to that which takes us away from closeness to our Creator. In Ramadan, we prayed extra prayers – now perhaps we are watching extra TV. In Ramadan, we gave extra charity – now perhaps we are doing a little extra shopping. In Ramadan, we protected our eyes and ears from sin, now perhaps we have celebrated Eid with a movie that included some inappropriate scenes. The world is splashing back at us, bits of *dunyā* splashing onto our hearts.

Once I went to a camp in the Poconos. It poured rain the whole time and the entire campsite was muddy. As I walked on the muddy paths, I looked carefully at every step. I avoid the richly muddy spots, and tried to place my feet in the "dryer" places. I stepped on slightly higher ground and skipped around the puddles. I still ended up with mud all over the bottom of my coat. I was, however, thankful that it was only in spots and that those are easily wiped away.

Walking on a footpath in the North of England, I wore Wellies and still managed to step into a deep bog of mud. I was pulled out, and wiped away the spray of mud that hit my face. I did not fully understand how to avoid the mud there, because large tufts of grass hide the dangerous, deep, sucking holes. I relied on my experienced English companions – actually I followed one and fell on the other! At the top of the hill, our original goal, I arrived covered in mud. My skirt had turned from navy blue to dark brown, and the coat I was meant to wear for my lectures the next day was covered in splotches of mud.

'Umar ﷦ was asked to define *taqwā,* and he said that it was the pulling up of one's skirts and watching where you walk.

Both of my walks in the mud were confirmations of this definition of *taqwā.* Indeed, we must avoid the spots that will suck us in, try to place our steps on a firm path of faith, and skip around all that is doubtful. Yet even if we do this, we will still end up splashed with sin and *dunyā.*

I used the shower and a washing machine to rid myself of the mud of my walks, but how are we to wipe away splashes of sin?

The Prophet ﷺ once said to his companions, "If one of you were to have a river in front of his door, that he washed in five times every day, would any dirt remain upon him?" They said, "There would be no dirt left upon him." And he ﷺ said, "So it is with the five daily prayers. Allah erases sin/misdeeds with them." (*Saḥīḥ Muslim*)

»أرأيتم لو أن نهرا بباب أحدكم يغتسل منه كل يوم خمس مرات، هل يبقى من درنه شيء؟" قالوا: لا يبقى من درنه شيء. قال "فذلك مثل الصلوات الخمس، يمحو الله بهن الخطايا.«

Thus it is that *taqwā* and careful steps in this *dunyā* will protect us from major sin, and our lesser sins and misdeeds can be easily wiped away with our prayers.

The obligatory prayers save us from the humiliation of

being covered in mud. As we slip and slide through this life, we often surprise ourselves with misplaced steps and unexpected falls. We must never skip an obligatory prayer because of a long highway commute, or 'no place to pray at work'. There is always time to stop and pray and there is always someplace to pray. When we miss a prayer, we leave a coating of mud on our spirits. Time after time, that mud may harden and remove the desire to pray all together.

The five prayers are our shower. They are our washing machine. They are our saving grace.

Let us walk carefully and pray regularly. Let us protect the *taqwā* gained in Ramadan, learn to walk gingerly through this *dunyā*, splash the least amount of sin back upon ourselves as possible and quickly clean off that which we cannot avoid. Let us never, ever allow the mud of sin and this *dunyā* to become a permanent feature of our spirits.

Reflection

Have you slipped back into the mud a bit after your Ramadan cleaning? Have bad habits begun to splash back a bit? Have you slipped into watching too much television? Neglecting Quran reading? Skipping *sunna* prayers?

Project

When the Quran talks about salat, it does not instruct us: Say your prayers. It instructs us to "Establish prayer…" Establishing prayer – setting up a habit of regular, on time meetings with Allah – feels entirely different than just "saying prayers". It builds a bond, a lifestyle, an identity. It keeps us attached by light and guidance to our Lord. It puts blessings in the time that comes after it. And it prevents us from straying too far or getting too dirty with the sin-splashes of the *dunyā*. This week, let us aim to pray our prayers – all five of them, every day – at the very beginning of the time. Each morning, check the prayer times schedule and plan your day so that you can pray all your prayers within the first fifteen minutes of the *adhān*. When it goes off, simply drop everything and rush to meet your Lord. Then write about the changes in your heart.

Tip

Making *wuḍūʾ* every time you visit the restroom helps because you are more likely to have *wuḍūʾ* when the salat comes in, and it is easier to jump up and do it!

Reflection / Project

Week 42

A Woman with a Voice

ASMĀ' BINT 'UMAYS 🌼 embraced Islam in its early years. In those years, Muslims were beaten to within an inch of their lives, their livelihood was cut off as Quraish interfered in their ability to buy and sell, and they lived in constant fear for their loved ones. But even all of this difficulty did not offset the emotional upheaval of the immigration to Abyssinia. They were in tormented anguish at the prospect of leaving their beloved Prophet 🌸. Speaking for all the Muslims who were setting out to migrate, 'Uthmān b. 'Affān said, "O Messenger of God, our first, and this – our second – migration to Negus and you are not with us?" to which their beloved responded, "You are immigrating to Allah and to me – both immigrations count for you." 'Uthmān responds with great decorum (adab), saying, "Then that suffices us, O Messenger of God." They were comforted by his words, as they left their hearts in his care.

Asmā' 🌼 made this journey to Abyssinia. She endured the days away from the Prophet 🌸 along with the rest of the Muslims. She adapted to her new environment and held on to her faith, growing in confidence and deepening in religion. In that faraway place, without the connecting graces of Facebook, Whatsapp, and Skype, she managed to remain true to Islam, loyal to her Prophet, and strong in faith.

Asmāʾ bint ʿUmays went to visit Ḥafṣa bint ʿUmar, Mother of the Believers, wife of the Prophet 鸞, after her long awaited return to Medina. While she was visiting, ʿUmar came to the house and, when he realized that she was Asmāʾ bint ʿUmays who had returned from Abyssinia by boat, he said, "We beat you to the *hijra*, and thus we have more of a right upon the Prophet 鸞 than you." Whatever motivated him to say this is unclear – Asmāʾ's reaction was, however, very clear. She was furious. It was an unbearable affront. All the years of missing the Prophet 鸞 and living in obedience to him could not mean that she – or any of her companions – had been beaten by anyone. She responded, "No, by God, you were with the Messenger of Allah, he fed you when you were hungry, and he educated you when you were in ignorance, and we were in a faraway and despicable land in Abyssinia – and we were there for God and His Prophet 鸞. By God I will not eat a morsel nor drink a drop until I tell the Messenger 鸞 what you have just said… And we were harmed and afraid! I will tell all of this to the Prophet 鸞 and I will ask him and by God I will not lie, nor trim, nor expand on what you said."

When the Prophet 鸞 came she said, "O Prophet of God! Verily ʿUmar has said such and such."

"And what did you say to him?" he asked

"I said, 'such and such.'"

He said, "He does not have more right upon me than you; for him and his companions are one *hijra* and for you, the people of the ship, are two *hijras*."

Asmāʾ's voice rang strong and true. She was not plagued with the depression of distance, nor was she too 'busy' to speak. She was not intimidated, and did not doubt her stance. She spoke to the Prophet 鸞, who listened and responded. Asmāʾ's choice to be heard became a source of joy for the people of the boat, and she herself tells us, "Abū Mūsā and the people of the ship would send me messengers asking about this hadith, and there is nothing more joyful or greater in this *dunyā* for them than what the Prophet ﷺ said about them." (*Ṣaḥīḥ al-Bukhārī*)

Her inner voice, vocalized, brought about a change in attitude and perspective.

Reflection

One of the issues in becoming 'mosqued' is enduring and interacting with unsolicited advice and criticism from other women at the mosque. Have you ever been the victim of such treatment? Were you able to respond with confidence and strength as Asmāʾ did? Or did it shake you and keep you away from the mosque?

Project

Stand up for yourself this week. Let your opinion and feelings be known when you feel bullied or "dissed." Be careful that in standing up for yourself you do not fall into the same critical or rude speech that you may have endured. Find your voice, speak with *taqwā*, and be confident in your words.

Reflection / Project

Week 43

A Call to Speak

RE OUR VOICES SILENCED by depression? Ignorance? Oppression? Are our voices made quiet by the distraction of 'busyness'? Lack of fervor? Self-indulgence? Or is it our very distance from Islam and our Prophet ﷺ that silences our voices?

Our missing voices indicate a deeply troubling reality. We are no longer drawn by conscience to any needs outside our own. Busy with personal problems that come and go like a sink of dishes, we do not reflect on our deeper callings. We have silenced our own voices.

Yet, we are faced with serious issues. Children who have lost their Muslim identity, refugees in need of Muslim 'cultural brokers'[1], converts who are 'de-converting' as they become disenchanted with the Muslim people in their lives. We have problems of domestic violence, incest, and other despicable sins that are not meant to be part of the lives of those who were called to 'enjoin the good and forbid the wrong'. With few exceptions, we are not talking about these problems. The silence is deafening.

As Muslim women, our missing voice has meant that we have allowed others to tell our stories. The story least

---

1 American friends who teach refugees what to accept and what to reject in American culture. (Pipher, *The Middle of Everywhere* pg.89)

heard is the story of the Muslim woman: missing is her happy story, her story of hard work and commitment, her story of love for the Prophet 🌷 and years of study, her story of overcoming hardship and reaching success. Missing also is the female voice in scholarship and activism based on the prophetic model, and missing is her voice against the wrongs done in the name of Islam.

It is time to end this state of affairs. It is time to stand up, cease being intimidated, cease being selfishly silent and cease leaving the speaking to others. It is time to find our voice.

Reflection

Where is your voice? Is it missing? Is there something you are speaking up about or out against? If not, what do you think is stopping you? Is there an issue you have always wanted to raise? How do you think you could go about raising it?

Project

One of the prerequisites for raising your voice is to be educated about your particular issue and about the related Islamic sciences and rulings. Spend some time this week planning for the expansion of your Islamic education, so that the foundation of your knowledge broadens and deepens, enabling you to speak from a more solid platform about any topic you're interested in. Consider enrolling in a Ribaat class for the upcoming semester. Rabata.org/ribaat

Reflection / Project

Week 44

Follow the Sound Waves of our Predecessors

A MUSLIM IS THE EPITOME of *adab*, and as such, finding our voices should not be an excuse for a shouting match or a reason to be nasty. Indeed, if we are to find our voices and use them effectively, we must follow the prophetic example.

✓ Do speak the truth and be kind, wise and confident.

Fāṭima bint Qais ﷺ had a unique ruling from the Prophet ﷺ regarding her divorce. She continued to narrate her hadith to the chagrin and downright disagreement of many, including ʿĀʾisha ﷺ and ʿUmar ﷺ. As a result, in the development of jurisprudence regarding marriage and divorce law, all four schools found a way to incorporate it into their law. Her story was not typical, but it was her story. Her voice made sure it was not an 'absent narrative.'

✓ Do volunteer; in our deeds is our loudest voice.

Fāṭima al-Fihriyya used the inheritance money she

received from her father to build the Qurawiyyīn mosque and university. Her work provided for the first formalized degree-granting institution *in the world.* Her voice encourages us to speak through deeds: building institutions, giving money, and creating vision.

✓ Do write for local papers and magazines, online and off. Write fiction books and non-fiction, poetry and real-life experiences.

Al-Khansā᾽ 🌼 was a poetess who was encouraged in her poetry by the Prophet 🌸. Before her Islam she wrote and recited famous poetry that lamented the deaths of her brothers in battle. After Islam, she continued to write – but as her worldview changed, so did her poetry. Her verses expressed the creative voice of one who saw the *ākhira* as a blessed reality to be sought. Her voice calls out to the world of literature and the written word – it calls us to put fingers to keyboard and express our voices on screens and paper everywhere.

✓ Do read widely and deeply so that you have something to say.

Nana Asma'u was a West African woman of profound scholarship and educational activism. Her home housed hundreds of hand-written volumes of sacred texts. The bookshelves included works on politics, Arabic, literature, and poetry. She was fluent in four languages and used her breadth of knowledge to build a network of female scholars and educators in West Africa in the nineteenth century. Her voice calls us to fill the empty places inside with knowledge and learning so that we too may be called forth to teach.

✓ Do speak up.

Umm Salama had a difficult series of *hijras*. She emigrated twice to Abyssinia, and then went out to emigrate to Medina, but was held back by her family. Her son was snatched out of her hands by his paternal kin, her husband went ahead on his *hijra* to Medina, and she was left in Mecca. When her son was finally released to her, she went forth on her final *hijra*, alone. She was reunited with her husband in Medina, and they began their life with the Prophet ﷺ. Perhaps because of her unique hardships, she longed to hear specifically about women and *hijra* in the Quran. She went to the Messenger ﷺ and said, "O Messenger of God, I do not hear God mentioning the women of the *hijra*." (*Sunan al-Tirmidhī*) She spoke up and was rewarded with revelation, as Allah ﷻ revealed to His messenger:

$$ فَٱسْتَجَابَ لَهُمْ رَبُّهُمْ أَنِّى لَآ أُضِيعُ عَمَلَ عَٰمِلٍ مِّنكُم مِّن ذَكَرٍ أَوْ أُنثَىٰ ۖ بَعْضُكُم مِّنْ بَعْضٍ ۚ $$

And their Lord answered them, "Never will I suffer to be lost the work of any of you, whether male or female; you are of one and another." (3:195)

Her voice calls out and says not to allow timidity to silence you, for in speaking up you may find a connection to your Creator that is overwhelming in its response.

Finding our voice will take practice. We must practice offering solutions that may be ignored and opinions that might be laughed at. Knowing our voice means knowing that we have a responsibility to speak. It means understanding that the potential we have been given must be tapped, for we will be asked why we left it dormant.

217

It is time to reach deeply within and find our voices once again. In the tradition of the women around the Prophet ﷺ, we must recognize our talents, find our enthusiasm for the roles Allah has given us, and take responsibility for our knowledge, our communities, and our *umma*.

Reflection

Is there a situation in your life where you have spoken up, but perhaps not in the wisest possible way? What are some ways you could communicate more effectively and more Islamically in future circumstances? If it is feasible and productive, contact the person you spoke to unwisely and try to make amends. If it is not, make *duʿāʾ* for them by name.

Project

Choose one area this week in which to raise your voice. Maybe you need to write a heartfelt, handwritten letter to a family member or design a course for new Muslims and propose teaching it at your masjid. Perhaps you feel called to write an article about an issue you hold dear or even start a blog to discuss a whole slew of issues. Maybe your voice needs to speak for those who have no voice, or stand up to forces – local or global – that would keep women uneducated or treat them as second-class citizens. Maybe it is poor people or the ill or the disabled you would like to assist in raising their own voices. Whatever it is, choose one way of raising your voice this week and write the results here.

Tip

As you warm up your voice, remember what Rūmī said, "Raise your words, not your voice. It is rain that grows flowers, not thunder." Keep all of your communications dignified and elegant, reflecting the highest level of *adab*.

Reflection / Project

Week 45

Use the Mute Button

A S WE PRACTICE FINDING our voice, we must be wary of the pitfalls of words that feel like voice, but are actually ego and are far from the *sunna* of our beloved Prophet ﷺ. Using our voices in these ways is not an authentic contribution to the betterment of society, but rather an exercise in self-righteous cacophony. Therefore:

✘ Do not complain and threaten to quit.

This was a habit of the hypocrites, one in which Abdullah b. Salūl was especially proficient. At the Battle of Uḥud, he drew away, taking three hundred soldiers with him. The reason he gave for deserting the Prophet ﷺ and his companions in their time of need? His opinion was ignored. He said, referring to the Prophet ﷺ, "He defied me and complied with young men and those who are not worthy of offering an opinion…"

How often are shouting matches begun because someone thinks his or her opinion is the only one that should be regarded as valid? How often are important projects dropped because committee members could not leave their egos at home? Knowing our own voice means recognizing the voice of others. It means authentic listening and putting aside of the ego. When our voice is used to complain or to create drama or to end good projects, we walk on the dangerous path of hypocrisy.

✗ Do not speak badly or poorly about anyone working for Allah.

Allah ﷻ says in *Sūrat al-Ḥujarāt*:

يَٰٓأَيُّهَا ٱلَّذِينَ ءَامَنُواْ ٱجْتَنِبُواْ كَثِيرًا مِّنَ ٱلظَّنِّ إِنَّ بَعْضَ ٱلظَّنِّ إِثْمٌ وَلَا تَجَسَّسُواْ وَلَا يَغْتَب بَّعْضُكُم بَعْضًا أَيُحِبُّ أَحَدُكُمْ أَن يَأْكُلَ لَحْمَ أَخِيهِ مَيْتًا فَكَرِهْتُمُوهُ وَٱتَّقُواْ ٱللَّهَ إِنَّ ٱللَّهَ تَوَّابٌ رَّحِيمٌ ﴿١٢﴾

O you who have believed, avoid much assumption. Indeed, some assumption is sin. And do not spy or backbite each other. Would one of you like to eat the flesh of his brother when dead? You would detest it. And fear Allah; indeed, Allah is Accepting of repentance and Merciful. (49:12)

Ibn ʿAsākir, in advising his brother, said, "And know, my brother... that the flesh of the scholar is poisonous." Be wary of the temptation to speak badly about people who are working for Allah ﷻ in any way. Finding fault and spreading rumors about people whose lives are dedicated to the preservation of God's religion is a treacherous road. It is not only divisive and dangerous for the community, but 'eating his/her flesh' is poison, and the using of one's own voice on the road to hellfire.

✗ Do not use your voice to gossip or tell other people's scandalous stories.

Abū Huraira narrates that the Prophet ﷺ said: "Do you know what *ghība* is?" They said, "Allah and His Messenger know best." He said: "Mentioning about your brother what he dislikes." Someone said: "And if what is said is true about my brother?" He said: "If what you say is true, you have committed *ghība* against him, and if it is not, you have slandered him." (*Ṣaḥīḥ Muslim*)

قال رسول الله صلى الله عليه وسلم: «أتدرون ما الغيبة؟» قالوا: الله ورسوله أعلم. قال «ذكرك أخاك بما يكره» قيل: أفرأيت إن كان في أخي ما أقول؟ قال «إن كان فيه ما تقول، فقد اغتبته. وإن لم يكن فيه، فقد بهته»

The best place for a gossipy story is nowhere. ʿĀʾisha, may Allah be pleased with her, suffered at the hands of gossip mongers and slander slingers. Her story is a painful reminder of the ugly places that words can take us as individuals and as a community. As Muslims we have enough people on Fox News and elsewhere competing in smear campaigns against us – we must not add our voices to that mix.

✗ Do not raise your voice to yell or shout or scream

Luqmān's advice to his son in the Quran is an Islamic rule of voice:

And be moderate in your pace and lower your voice; indeed, the most disagreeable of sounds is the voice of donkeys. (31:19)

We are not a people who shout in the mosque or yell at women or scream at children. The voice that Allah gave us should be used to comfort, spread joy and bring smiles. When our voices are used to admonish and advise, they should carry with them the respect found in low and quiet tones. Anas b. Mālik ﷺ tells us, "Allah did not send a prophet except with a beautiful face and a beautiful voice, and your prophet was the best of face and voice." We are called to imitate the example found in our beloved Prophet ﷺ, and thus we must work to have a beautiful voice – one that is easy on the ears and does not irritate or antagonize. The Quran is very clear; our voice must not become as the braying of a donkey.

✗ Do not speak for the sole purpose of hearing yourself talk – each word should be measured and have a goal.

Ibn ʿUmar ﷺ narrates that the Prophet ﷺ said: Do not be excessive in words, other than in the remembrance of Allah, for excessive talk without the remembrance of Allah hardens the heart, and the farthest of people from Allah is the hard hearted. (*Sunan al-Tirmidhī*)

«لا تكثر الكلام بغير ذكر الله، فان كثرة الكلام بغير ذكر الله قسوة للقلب، وان أبعد الناس من الله القلب القاسي.»

The committee meetings wherein members argue again and again about issues that have already been beaten down with a stick are some of the most painful places to be. Voices are not used to thoughtfully find solutions, but to show off to others that one is "smart, too" or even "smarter".

The Muslim's worldview is knitted to the concept of *ḥisāb*, or being held to account. We recognize that each word we say is written, either for us or against us. Even in this *dunyā*, our words never disappear. Their sound waves go out into the universe where they hold record of every word we have ever said.

Finding our voice implies finding meaning. Our words must be rooted to a deeper goal – the goal that helped us find our voice in the first place.

Reflection

How well do you hear yourself? It can be very easy to hear the complaining and shouting of other people, but miss it completely within ourselves. What grade might you give yourself in this area? Think about it and then do the project below.

Project

Keep a record in the chart below of times you should have chosen the mute button this week. Just tally up the number. Did you do better or worse than expected? What might you do to improve your self control when it comes to the words you say?

	Friday	Saturday	Sunday	Monday	Tuesday	Wednesday	Thursday
Complained							
Found Fault							
Gossiped							
Shouted							
Talked in Excess							

Reflection / Project

_____
_____
_____
_____
_____
_____
_____
_____
_____
_____
_____
_____
_____
_____
_____
_____
_____
_____
_____

Week 46

Fight the Brain Drain

HE PROPHET ﷺ SAID, "A single *faqīh* (one who is learned in religion) is more brutal to Shaiṭān than one thousand worshippers." (*Sunan Ibn Māja*)

«فقيه واحد أشدّ عَلَى الشيطان من ألف عابد.»

And Allah ﷻ says, *...God will raise those of you who believe and those of you who have gained knowledge by degrees...* (58:11)

يَرْفَعِ ٱللَّهُ ٱلَّذِينَ ءَامَنُواْ مِنكُمْ
وَٱلَّذِينَ أُوتُواْ ٱلْعِلْمَ دَرَجَتٍ

The rank of the learned is great.

One of the most distinctive characteristics of people who are knowledgeable on any subject is that they claim to know very little. Knowing more always, without exception, opens doors that remind us of how little we actually know.

As women, we often get sidetracked and allow our brains to become comfortably squishy with oatmeal and kitchen sponges. We must fight this very literal 'brain drain' (does it run out in the shower?) with a vigorous program of learning.

We must read new material every day. We must enroll in classes (one per semester is enough – even one a year is better than zero). We must discuss new ideas, read the newspaper, watch the news. We must learn about our religion and learn about the world around us.

Life is not going to get easier or less busy. Every year will bring new trials and new blessings, all of which will fill our days and nights. We must set our feet firmly on a path of learning, and then take strides upon it.

What to Learn and How

1. Things we know nothing about and we know we know nothing about: Read children's books. They are a wonderful resource for non-scientists to learn biology and the miracle of chemistry. If you are a scientist branching out into poetry, a book written for a fifth grader will give you plenty to start with.

2. Things we think we know everything about: Take a class from a professional teacher or read an academic book or journal article. Take the fifty books per year challenge and read (just about) one book per week. Join a book club or discuss books online. Stretch your brain cells and increase your learning curve.

3. Language learning: We need to increase our vocabulary every day – and this includes English (or your native language). Words are thoughts. The more words we have, the better we will think and understand. With more understanding comes deeper faith. We also need to learn Arabic. This is a no-excuse subject. This is the language of the Quran. And if you think you already know it well enough, see #2.

Our *umma*, our communities, our families need the blessing of knowledgeable people. Yaḥyā b. Muʿādh (may God have mercy on him) said, "The scholars are a greater mercy to the *umma* of Muhammad than their mothers and fathers." It was asked, "How is that?" He said, "Because the fathers and mothers protect them from the fire of this world, but the scholars protect them from the fire of the afterlife."

Be a mercy to the *umma* of the merciful one 鐃 sent by the Most Merciful 鐃. Make a learning plan today.

Reflection

Is there an area that you are an expert in? Are you a knitter? A cyclist? An amateur astronomer? Do you know how to make your own yoghurt? Understand First Nation history? Sew like there is no tomorrow? If you have a specialty, how are you using it currently? Have you put it on the shelf or are you using it to serve Islam? If you do not have a specialty, what area would you like to delve into?

Project

Pick something you have always wanted to learn about. It could be the cosmos, gardening, the history of martial arts, whatever you are interested in. Set a task this week to find out as much about that topic as you can.

Reflection / Project

_____

_____

_____

_____

_____

_____

_____

_____

_____

_____

_____

_____

_____

_____

_____

_____

_____

_____

_____

_____

Week 47

Respect

THE PROPHET ﷺ SAID, "He is not of my *umma*, who does not honor/respect our elders, have mercy on our young and know the right of our scholars." (*Musnad al-Imām Aḥmad*)

«ليس من أمّتي من لم يجلّ كبيرنا
ويرحم صغيرنا ويعرف لعالمنا حقّه.»

These are strong words. When we look at the life of the Prophet ﷺ and see how gently he spoke to people, and then we come back to this sentence, "He is not of my *umma*..." we begin to understand the gravity of this particular hadith.

In modern terms, what does it mean? Does it mean we no longer play for his ﷺ team? We are no longer of the 'Muslim' nationality? We do not belong to a particular club?

"He is not of my *umma*..." The Prophet ﷺ begins his admonition with this phrase of exclusion – the ticket to isolation from the greatest and best group that ever walked the earth. Here the Prophet ﷺ emphasizes the seriousness, not of an action, but of an attitude.

Often I am asked by women around the world about difficult relationships with their children, their parents, their husbands, their bosses, their imams, etc. And universally, what I find is that the core of the problem is not a deed but rather a stance.

With children, women are often frustrated with their behavior, and they ask me for magic pills to turn them into model Muslims. But asked, "How does your child feel?" the answer is usually difficult to come by. When we do not know how our children feel, we are not merciful to them. When we set high expectations and do not think about their feelings along the way, we frustrate them. Our job is to teach and guide, to be sure, but how much teaching and guiding have you ever welcomed into your life from a person who looked upon you with eyes devoid of mercy?

When it comes to our elders, western Muslims struggle. The word respect is defined differently in Western societies. In a place where college professors are called by their first names, children raise their voices to their parents and equality has been taken to a pathological level, our elders suffer the most.

I recently rode in the car with a seventy-year-old woman; she is highly educated and has contributed much in her life to her field and her community. She said to me, "I need to work on understanding my new role in society." I asked what that new role was, and she replied, "I'm old now – and the young do not want my perspective anymore." Ouch.

Some of the most beautiful aspects of Islamic culture are the trappings of respect. Standing up when someone enters a room, sitting with decent posture in front of those who are our elders and holding our tongue more often than it wants to be held.

But in the end, it is not the deeds of respect that the Prophet ﷺ was speaking of; it is the attitude.

So let us take heed of the Prophet ﷺ. Do not belittle or look down upon your parents, your husband, or anyone older than you. Be vigilant about this. Ask yourself about your real attitude towards anyone you have a relationship problem with, and you will probably find that at its core is your own heart full of disparaging thoughts and feelings.

Let us attempt to 'feel' the feelings of those who are younger, as we guide them with the loving hand of mercy toward a life of faith. Let us honor our elders and remove all traces of belittling from our hearts.

Indeed, in this way we will find peace in our homes, in our communities, in our organizations and in our hearts. Our relationship with Allah ﷻ will improve and our faith will deepen.

And when we remember the words of the Prophet ﷺ, we will be able to say, "I am, O dear beloved Messenger, I am one of yours. I am a part of your beautiful *umma*."

Reflection

Sometimes we look upon someone in our life as a burden or an obstacle, instead of as a real person with ideas, needs and frailties of his or her own. Are you frustrated when your peers or your elders do not behave the way you think they should? Are you missing out on opportunities to gain Allah's pleasure by serving your parents or in-laws or being extra kind to the elderly aunties? Using sarcasm against your children when they don't toe the line? Perhaps most painfully, have you given up on your husband because he does not meet the expectations you had when you married? What do you think are the origins of these feelings?

Project

Although it is not recognized in our modern, Western culture, very often in life actions come before feelings. Just like making *dhikr* and increasing *ʿibāda* usually come before feelings of spiritual peace and growth, so behaving in a positive manner toward someone can precede actual positive feelings about him/her. This week, try behaving in a respectful manner toward someone you feel you should respect more. Greet them warmly, open a door for them, stand when they enter the room, etc. These outer trappings of respect can soften your own heart as well as theirs, and even if their behavior does not change, you will have changed your relationship from a source of frustration and disrespect into an act of worship that will allow you to concentrate on pleasing Allah rather than resenting the other person.

Reflection / Project

Week 48

Days of Change

$\mathcal{T}$HE TEN DAYS OF Dhū al-Ḥijja swirl and roll around us like leaves on invisible wind currents. Islam is a religion that provides us with seasons of opportunity. The season of hajj is an opportunity for renewal.

The actual pilgrimage is an obligation upon every Muslim man and woman. There are specific rites and duties that every Muslim will participate in. The *saʿī*, or passing back and forth between Ṣafā and Marwā, is the honoring of the action of Hājar, who, when left alone in the desert with her son did not passively sit back and await Allah's help, nor did she panic and seek her own human solution. Rather, she demonstrated pure and absolute *tawakkul*: complete confidence in Allah's ﷻ solution and willingness to put forth her best effort to bring it about. All Muslims who go on hajj and/or *ʿumra* will find themselves imitating her and honoring her. It is a powerful message.

Historically, the hajj was an arduous trip that could take months and would often change the course of people's lives. We hear stories of those who went to hajj and, upon their visit to Medina, could not bear to leave and so remained. We hear stories of those who fell ill and did not recover. And we hear stories of great and permanent repentance. The hajj is a multi-faceted season.

The Prophet 🕊 said, "There are no days more beloved to God that He be worshiped in them than the ten days of Dhū al-Ḥijja. Each day of fasting in it is equivalent to the fast of an entire year. And each night standing in prayer is equivalent to standing in prayer on the Night of Power." (*Sunan al-Tirmidhī*)

«ما من أيام أحب إلى الله أن يتعبد له فيها من عشر ذي الحجة يعدل صيام كل يوم منها بصيام سنة وقيام كل ليلة منها بقيام ليلة القدر.»

The millions of Muslims who do not go on hajj are not deprived of the blessings of these days. Their fasting and their praying are generously rewarded. It is an opportunity for habit changing, to extend ourselves and discover what feats of worship we are capable of.

It is an opportunity to imitate Hājar in absolute trust. As she was left alone in the desert to seek sustenance for herself and her child, we often feel alone in the world. We must seek our sustenance in our belief, in our faith, and in our religion. With full trust in Allah 🕊 that He can fill our lonely spaces, we must put forth our very best effort. The road to Allah 🕊 has been paved by the Prophet 🕊, and in prayer, *dhikr*, *duʿāʾ*, Quran reading and fasting we find ourselves on his smoothed and well-tended road.

For 'pilgrims at home' – those of us who were not invited to the sacred House this year but wish to take full advantage of the blessings of these days – the ten days of Dhū al-Ḥijja will pass quickly. We are surrounded by our children, obligated to go to work and still involved in the daily grind. We may feel disconnected from the entire hajj.

The game 'Pilgrims at Home' is one way to join others and benefit from this season of the hajj and pull our family members and community members into the blessing of the season along with us.

The days of Dhū al-Ḥijja color our spirits and rejuvenate our hearts. Each one of the ten days is a bucket of paint ready to brighten our dull spaces and spruce up our shabby corners. A blessed few will be called to visit the sacred House. They will spend these days going around the Kaʿba and fulfilling the rites of hajj. When they return, they will return new and fresh, cleansed of sin and ready to start anew.

Every day is a new beginning and a new chance to do your best – in the 'Pilgrims at Home' game and in this 'game' of life. Indeed, as Imām al-Shāfiʿī said, "O child of Ādam, you are but a gathering of days, when one leaves, a piece of you leaves as well."

So let us look with joyful eyes upon our days and embrace whatever they have to offer. Let us use our hardships to gain patience and closeness and our blessings to gain thankfulness and closeness. Let every day be a day of closeness.

As we work to imitate Hājar, let our hajj story be one of legend. Whether at home or at the House, let us create deep and permanent change. Let us find our permanent sustenance and fulfill our deepest needs. *Āmīn.*

Reflection

If you have been on hajj, reflect on the way you felt immediately upon your return. What were the lessons that so vividly presented themselves to you and that you vowed to live by in the future? Are you living up to that vow?

If you have not been, examine your feelings about going on hajj. Does it feel like something distant and nebulous, not really attainable? Or is it something you intensely long for? Make *duʿāʾ* that Allah will put the longing in your heart and will facilitate a way to fulfill it. Take the first step by setting firm your intention – that when you have the ability and the means, you will make that journey.

Project

It is often difficult for those of us at home to feel the joy and blessings of the hajj season, but they are indeed raining down upon us all. Join a Pilgrims at Home team or download the Pilgrims at Home game manual from Rabata.org and try to incorporate as many of the *ʿibāda* activities as you can into your days this week. They will enable you to make the most of the opportunity of these ten days.

Reflection / Project

Week 49

The Day of ʿArafa

THE PROPHET ﷺ SAID, "THERE is no day more venerable to God than the Day of ʿArafa. God descends to the heavens of the earth and exalts the people of the earth to the inhabitants of the heavens. He says: "Look at my servants, disheveled, dusty and tired. They have come from every far-off corner of the earth. They have not witnessed My mercy and they have not witnessed My punishment. And I do not see a day in which more people are saved from the hellfire than the Day of ʿArafa." (*Majmaʿ al-Zawāʾid*)

«ما من يوم أفضل عند الله من يوم عرفة ينزل الله إلى السماء
الدنيا فيباهي بأهل الأرض أهل السماء فيقول: انظروا إلى
عبادي شعثاً غبراً صاحين جاؤوا من كل فج عميق ولم يروا رحمتي
ولم يروا عذابي، فلم أر يوماً أكثر عتيقاً من النار من يوم عرفة.»

And Ibn ʿUmar ﷺ reports that the Prophet ﷺ said, "When the evening of ʿArafa arrives, nobody with a mustard seed's weight of faith in their hearts is left, but that they are forgiven." It was said, "O Messenger of God, is this only for the people standing on ʿArafa?" He said, "No. It is for all the Muslims." (*Majmaʿ al-Zawāʾid*)

«إذا كان عشية عرفة لم يبق أحد في قلبه مثقال حبة من خردل من الإيمان إلا غفر له، قيل: يا رسول الله أهل عرفة خاصة؟ قال: بل للمسلمين عامة.»

Stand still. Close your eyes and imagine yourself standing on the plain of ʿArafa. All around you are men and women of every skin color, every economic class, every educational level, every possible category of the human being. Each one stands before Allah ﷻ with hands held high, palms facing up, head bent down, asking for her deepest needs and most fervent hopes. And each one needs most the hope of forgiveness.

The day of ʿArafa should not be an ordinary day. Clear your schedule. Plan to spend time in solidarity with those who stand on the plain of ʿArafa.

The Prophet ﷺ has said that the fasting on the day of ʿArafa is an expiation of the sins of the previous year and the upcoming year. (*Ṣaḥīḥ Muslim*)

«صِيَامُ يَوْمِ عَرَفَةَ أَحْتَسِبُ عَلَى اللهِ أَنْ يُكَفِّرَ السَّنَةَ الَّتِي قَبْلَهُ وَالسَّنَةَ الَّتِي بَعْدَهُ.»

This particular gift is especially for the pilgrim at home – those of us who are standing in our living rooms and not on the plain of ʿArafa.

This one twenty-four hour period can bring about great change. Wherever you are, seek forgiveness, make *duʿāʾ* and plead with your Lord. I remember one day of ʿArafa some years ago; I had invited a number of women to my house to spend the day in worship and prayer. After reading Quran and spending time in the meritorious phrases of the day of ʿArafa, we joined together in prayer and made some very personal requests of our Generous Lord. One of the women had been trying to conceive for many years, and was about to try IVF for the first and only time. She was a woman of great faith and trust, and was ready to resign herself to not having children, but felt that it was important for her future psyche to exhaust every possibility. So she and her husband had decided to try IVF just once. For many couples, trying to conceive via IVF becomes almost an addiction as they do it again and again, unable to accept that their destiny may not be in parenthood. As we made *duʿāʾ* together, we asked in hope (and perhaps in a bit of giddy excitement about the possibilities of the day of ʿArafa), that she be granted not one child, but three. We prayed for triplets. Today those three children are in school – three beautiful answered prayers of the day of ʿArafa.

We all need forgiveness, and we all rely on our Lord to fulfill our deepest hopes. The day of ʿArafa is a once a year opportunity. Seize the day. Seize the opportunity. Seize the day of ʿArafa.

Reflection

Arafa is like the Day of Judgment, in that all the pilgrims are standing alone together before their Lord – everyone equal and everyone in need of Him. Imagine yourself standing on that final Day with your book of deeds in your hand, ready to review it in front of your Lord. What things would you be ashamed to present? What things would you be proud to display? Make *duʿāʾ* this week that Allah will help you with your specific challenges, cover your sins on that day and enable you to excel in the things that please Him.

Project

Project – clear out your schedule on the Day of ʿArafa– plan to fast if you can – dedicate the day or at least a chunk of the day to worship. Make *du'ā'*, talk to Allah for a sustained period of time. If you struggle with *du'ā'*, use a *du'ā'* book to help prompt you. You may find there are ones you are drawn to – repeat them, add to them, ponder them. Sit down beforehand and make a list of things you need guidance on, wish to ask for, or are thankful for. Let this day of repentance and worship cleanse you and reboot your intentions going forward. Check the worship schedule for the day of 'Arafa in the Pilgrims at Home guide book and plan to implement as much as you can.

Reflection / Project

Week 50

Eid Again!

T IS EID! EID Mubārak! Eid Karīm! May every year bring with it health, goodness and blessings.

Eid al-Aḍḥā is a very meaningful celebration for our *umma*. We celebrate our brothers and sisters who find themselves invited to His house – to the Kaʿba. We celebrate their *tawba*, their repentance. We celebrate their dedication to their religion. We celebrate their willingness to sacrifice money and time in order to fulfill the rite of hajj.

For those at hajj, who will return to us, it is upon them to bring back their renewed sense of faith. To spread that goodness throughout the world – in all the villages, towns and cities represented in Mecca and Medina today.

For those of us at home, it is upon us to build a world that will receive those who come back from the hajj with the open arms of sisterhood and support.

We are celebrating our role as inheritors of the legacy of Ibrāhīm ﷺ. Look around your town, your city, your neighborhood – what do you see? We are surrounded by those who are also descendants of that legacy. It may be forgotten or buried or even ignored – but every person of The Book is part of the same legacy.

We must take the impetus of these days of hajj and reach out to people around us. Spread the goodness that is the message of Islam. Do something surprisingly good.

Yesterday I went to a local doughnut shop and, after choosing one of almost every type of doughnut in the store, I went to pay and glimpsed a sign that was hidden behind the pen jar: "Cash Only." Oh no. I actually said that out loud. "Oh no! You only take cash?" as I began to rummage through my purse.

At that moment two women walked into the store. They breezed in with the smile reserved for a doughnut store, the smile that says, "I'm about to eat a doughnut." They heard me, and one of them said, "Oh, we can buy your doughnuts." She smiled and I was aghast.

Having lived in Syria for twenty years, I was distraught at the very idea of someone paying for my doughnuts. Not to mention that I had plenty of money for those doughnuts, but it was all tied up in the plastic card I held in my hand.

"No, no!" I said, "I'll run to the ATM, I'll be right back."

They were cheerful and smiley and insistent. I said, "You don't know how many doughnuts I just bought." At which she plopped all her cash down on the counter and said, "Well this can go toward them." She had $18 and my doughnuts were $15.

She did not tell me to believe in Jesus, or that God loves me. She was just doing a nice thing. Indeed, in an attempt to make me feel better about it she said, "Your card is from the bank that I work at; consider it a gift from your bank."

Finally, the owner, who spoke very little English, got involved and forced me to take their good will. So I did.

I walked out of the store, put my doughnuts in the car, and spied my *dhikr* counter. I had just been reciting *al-ṣalawāt al-Ibrāhīmiyya*, and it struck me that we Muslims pray for humanity in every *farḍ* prayer when we ask that Allah ﷻ bless and sanctify the families of Muhammad and Ibrāhīm.

I prayed for those two women. I prayed they would be blessed with guidance as a reward for their very kind deed. And I prayed for us. I prayed that we Muslim women would be of the people of really good deeds: Deeds that stand out in people's memories; deeds that change the lives of the people around us; deeds that support our Muslim sisters and their families, and deeds that support our Abrahamic sisters and their families.

Yā Rabb. Make this Eid be the Eid we link arms together and begin to live in the shelter of each other, that we may extend that shelter to the women around us.

Āmīn.

Reflection

Can you remember a time that someone treated you to a random act of kindness? How did it make you feel? Did you pay it forward? Conversely, can you remember how you felt when you offered someone else an act of kindness?

Project

Make it your goal this week to perform a random act of kindness every single day. It does not have to be earth-shattering, just a small gesture. It can be done openly, like the doughnut ladies, or kept between you and Allah. Put money in someone's parking meter, leave flowers on someone's doorstep, pay for the meal of the car behind you in the drive thru. Write about the joy your kindness brings to you and its recipient (if you know them or see it!)

Reflection / Project

Week 51

Projections

WHEN I WAS YOUNG, my parents would show home movies every once in a while. It meant the digging out of 8 mm films, a screen and a projector. We would then sit and watch my young mother and father smile and wave at the camera. They were silent movies, so we could speak freely and laugh about my mother's hairstyle or my crooked smile.

On that screen was a projection.

We, as Muslims, have to learn to recognize projections and grow past them, into real believers.

The new 'global culture' is so deeply entrenched in selfishness, desirability, and comfort that it is difficult for us to identify the projections we make. But we are making them. And unlike the screen projections of my childhood, these projections distort reality and stand as barriers to our growth.

We project onto our family members how we think they feel, we project onto our communities what we see and hold them accountable when they fail to meet our expectations, and most dangerously, we project onto our spiritual path and upbringing, insisting that it takes us where we think we should go, by the route we think should get us there.

A Muslim women might put on hijab and expect that the result will be "enlightenment" – or at least ease. Then when her husband objects or her friends mock, she wonders why "Allah has 'done this to her,' since she did what was right." She may take it off and blame Islam, Muslims and God for her previous misery. This is a projection. Instead of dealing with the inner spiritual problem she has – one of low self-esteem, lack of commitment to God's law and the need for the approval of people – she projects her problems onto Islam and gets angry.

In another scenario, a Muslim woman chooses to wake up for *tahajjud*, but she finds difficulty. She is tired and crabby, and looks with a jealous eye on others' lifestyles. "If only I wasn't married/was married and did not have young children/had young children, I would be able to wake up." Or she might say, "If I had a job/did not have a job, I could get up for *tahajjud*." She doesn't look deeply within herself to analyze and eradicate that which is making it difficult, but rather judges by her projection, which says, "If I wake up for *tahajjud*, I should feel awakened – physically and spiritually." So she gives it up and smiles knowingly when asked, saying, "It just wasn't working for me."

Some Muslim women begin on a spiritual path, projecting their "fast food mentality" to the teacher and/or method. When they do not find immediate enlightenment, when it dawns on them that this is going to take work – a lot of it – they leave. They wanted a pill, not a life plan. Others expect to be given a litany of worship, and they jump head first into the lap of a teacher, expecting the 'prescription'. If the teacher says the unexpected – instead of "Do *dhikr*," she says, "Give money to your mother," or, "Get a job," or "Go back to school," – the student balks. This is not the way it is "supposed to be." In this projection the student has an image in her head of what the path looks like, and wants to be able to brag to friends about long litanies –

not about extra laundry or more hours at work. Here, instead of going deeply within to iron out the wrinkles of her personality, she doubts the teacher and sometimes the path. She often returns to the "Mall of Shaikhs" – looking for one who will "do it right."

Projections distort our thinking. As they increase, we become more self-righteous and farther from the path of deep faith. One way to check for a projection is to gauge our emotional reactions. Very often, our strongest negative reactions are not because the other person is acting inappropriately, but rather because we have projected onto him our own expectations. That is why when some guy in Walmart bumps into you and says 'excuse me' – we smile and say, 'That's ok'. But if a Muslim bumps into us at the local mosque, we get irritated and spend many days lamenting the state of Muslims, belittling them and complaining about their *adab*.

And while complaining fills the *nafs* with satisfaction (because it shifts blame to other than you), it does not put the hijab back on, it does not wake us up at night to pray and it does not make us people of *adab*.

We must be willing to pull back our projections and take an honest look at our deep inner weaknesses.

Carl Jung said, "Everything that irritates us about others can lead us to an understanding of ourselves." In understanding ourselves, we can remove the projections we build up to protect ourselves from effective, deep work.

Abū Bakr ﷺ said that the Prophet ﷺ said, "Hold tight to '*Lā ilāha illā Allah*' and the asking of God's forgiveness, and repeat them often. For Iblīs has said, 'I caused the people's ruin with sin, and they caused my ruin with "*Lā ilāha illā Allah*" and the asking of God's forgiveness. When I saw that, I caused their ruin by making them follow their desires while thinking that they were guided.'" (*Kanz al-ʿUmmāl*)

«عليكم بلا إله إلا الله والاستغفار، فأكثروا منهم فإن إبليس قال: أهلكت الناس بالذنوب، وأهلكوني بلا إله إلا الله والاستغفار، فلما رأيت ذلك أهلكتهم بالأهواء، وهم يحسبون أنهم مهتدون.»

In ending our projections, we move away from the whisperings of Shaiṭān.

Once we are able to look ourselves in the mirror and see the person in the reflection for who she truly is, once we stop projecting our own problems and expectations onto our families, community and path, at that point we can become the *umma* we were meant to be. People of light. People who live as the companions of the Prophet ﷺ lived. People who truly believe and whose good deeds are like joyful rain to the parched earth.

Reflection

One of the most common afflictions of people who are beginning to grow religiously is that they suddenly begin to judge everyone else through the prism of their new knowledge, instead of concentrating on judging themselves. Whenever they read Islamic advice or injunctions, they immediately think, "Yeah! My husband sure needs to hear this one!" or "I wish my mother obeyed that one!" Breaking this habit and seeing your own faults before those of others begins when you are able to identify and eliminate (or at least diminish) the projections that are flickering through your relationships. Sift through your relationships and examine them for projections. What are the deeper issues within yourself that the projections are masking?

Project

Projections are a tool of Shaiṭān, and one of the best weapons against Shaiṭān is the *tahlīl* (*lā ilāha illā Allah*). Set a goal this week for 70,000 repetitions of la ilaha illa Allah. Spend time in the morning and the evening in quiet meditation on these words. Take note of any insight you achieve.

Reflection / Project

_____

_____

_____

_____

_____

_____

_____

_____

_____

_____

_____

_____

_____

_____

_____

_____

_____

_____

_____

_____

_____

_____

Week 52

Feats of Felicity

GREAT EXHILARATING FEELINGS COME from great accomplishments.

When Barak Obama won the presidency in 2009 the faces of his supporters streamed with tears of unbelievable euphoria.

When Gotze scored the winning goal for Germany in the 2014 World Cup, his face spoke pure joy.

When my husband's grandmother graduated from college and published her first book at eighty-two-years old, her smile beamed brighter than the stage lights.

For Muslims, our celebrations are rooted in accomplishments. The Eid of Ramadan is a celebration of our individual fulfillment of the pillar of fasting, and the Eid of Hajj is a celebration of our *umma* and the people who were able to fulfill the pillar of pilgrimage. The joy on these days is rooted in the feeling of accomplishment.

As we come to the close of the *hijrī* year 1436, and look back upon our accomplishments, I pray that we will be hit with the giddy joy of true growth. It is a fitting moment of celebration.

Imam al-Ghazālī, referring to the importance of self-reflection, says, "When you have obtained that seed of happiness, place those (tools) underfoot and turn your face to the resting place of your own happiness, that resting place for which the elite expression is the Divine presence and for which the common expression is Paradise. All these matters must be learned so that you may know a little about yourself. The prize of the Way of Religion for whoever does not come to know these is like husks, and he is deprived of the true nature [and best part] of religion."

After twelve months of self-reflection and hard work, you have obtained the seed of happiness: plant it. Plant it within your own heart and continue on the road to God. Plant it in your family and help them to a life of Islam and the clean and loving living that is a result of adherence to the legal limits of religion. Plant it in your community and stretch your arms to care for and support the youth, the elders and the needy. Plant it in the *umma*, that we may once again rise up and be of the best of people, calling to that which is good and wholesome and true and rising above all that is ugly and poisonous and false.

The joy of faith is true. I pray it rings loud and clear in the lives of all of you, your families, your friends and communities.

I pray that our joy will be manifest on the day when there is no joy but the joy that comes from deeds that were done for Allah ﷻ. I pray that on that day, our faces will beam brightly, will speak of pure joy and unbelievable euphoria. I pray that we will hear the words of our Lord as He says,

O contented soul, return to your Lord, well pleased and pleasing, and enter among My servants and enter My Paradise. (89:28-30)

ٱرْجِعِى إِلَى رَبِّكِ رَاضِيَةً مَّرْضِيَّةً ۝ فَٱدْخُلِى فِى عِبَٰدِى ۝ وَٱدْخُلِى جَنَّتِى ۝

Āmīn.

Reflection

Think back to your relationships of a year ago - your relationship with Allah and your relationships with others. Where were you? How have you changed?

Project

Look back through this journal, taking note of each of the weekly projects. How many did you complete? How many of the habits have you continued? Write down three ways in which you have changed this year. They don't have to be huge changes - perhaps it was a shift in the way you interacted with your mother-in-law, perhaps it was the introduction of an extra *sunna* prayer... All of these are progress. All of these call for celebration.

May Allah reward you for every ounce of effort you put into purifying your actions and intentions this year. May your extra deeds be a light for you on your path towards Him and comforting companions on the Day of Judgment. May your steps forward be easy, may your habits take root and affect those around you and may this year to come be a year of further growth and closeness to Allah and those He loves.

Āmīn.

Reflection / Project

About the Author

ANSE TAMARA GRAY IS the founder of *Rabata*, an organization dedicated to promoting positive cultural change through individual empowerment, the spiritual upbringing of women by women, and the revival of the female voice in scholarship.

Anse Tamara lived in Syria for twenty years, studying sacred knowledge and traveling along the road of *tarbiya* (spiritual upbringing). She studied a full curriculum of Islamic sacred texts and subjects including: Shāfiʿī jurisprudence (*fiqh*), Islamic theology (*ʿaqīda*), Quranic sciences (*tafsīr* and *tajwīd*), Arabic grammar (*naḥū*), geography of the Muslim world, Islamic civilization and culture, Islamic history, and classical methods of spiritual growth (*tazkiya*). Her specialty is the life of the Prophet, peace and blessings be upon him (*sīra*), which she studied in-depth with the foremost *sīra* scholar of our time. She is fluent in both spoken and classical Arabic and received her *ijāza* in the recitation of Quran from the late Shaikh Muḥyī al-Dīn al-Kurdī in 1997.

Anse Tamara is a doctoral student in the Leadership, Policy and Administration program at the University of St. Thomas in St. Paul, MN. She holds a master's degree in Curriculum Theory and Instruction and works in the field of education, focusing on instruction, curriculum design, and implementation, administration, and teacher training. Her publications range from several culturally appropriate English language curriculum programs to translations of sacred texts.

Some of the projects she has initiated through *Rabata* include: *The Lina Project*, a two-day workshop that addresses the unique needs of female converts; *Circles of Light*, group and individual activities that foster a strong habit of worship; *Daybreak* a publishing company and third space in Minnesota, and *Ribaat*, an online academic program that brings college-level Islamic learning to women across the world.

Notes

Notes

Notes

Notes

Contest

*T*he **New Day Rabata Writers Contest** offers you an opportunity to be heard. Your voice is important, your story matters, and your knowledge can make a difference. Send us your manuscript today!

Daybreak Press seeks to publish the works of previously unpublished female authors with the launch of its New Day annual writing contest.

Topics rotate yearly from poetry to fiction to nonfiction. For 2015, we will be accepting fiction submissions. The deadline for submissions is December 31 each year, and winners will be announced each March.

Grand prize – A publishing package from Daybreak Press that includes author support, professional editing services, typesetting, ISBN assignment, cover design, etc., and a cash prize of $500.00.

For more information please visit http://www.rabata.org/daybreak. We look forward to reading your stories!

DAYBREAK PRESS

DAYBREAK PRESS

AYBREAK PRESS is the publishing arm of Rabata, an international organization dedicated to promoting positive cultural change through the spiritual mentoring of women by women and the revival of the female voice in scholarship. Daybreak is committed to publishing female scholars, activists, and authors in the genres of poetry, fiction and non-fiction. It sponsors the annual New Day writing contest for unpublished female authors and operates the Daybreak Bookstore in St. Paul, Minnesota. For more information please visit Rabata.org/Daybreak.

DAYBREAK PRESS